IBERIA

by

BIKE

WORK DESK TO WILD CAMP

IBERIA
by
BIKE

A MERRY RIDE ROUND

WORK DESK TO WILD CAMP

Exploring France, Spain and Portugal on a motorbike

JIM MERRYFIELD

First published by A Merry Ride Round, October 2021

ISBN pbk 978-1-7399032-0-6
ISBN ebk 978-1-7399032-1-3

Design and typesetting www.ShakspeareEditorial.org
Illustrations Whereabouts Maps
Cover design More Visual

Warning: this book contains the use of swearing

A Merry Ride Round

Tag **@amerryrideround** on Instagram or Facebook with a photo of you and this book and the **#amerryrideround #amrr #iberiabybike** hashtags.

www.amerryrideround.com

As much as I love the idea of this book perched gracefully upon your shelf, considering that the theme of this book is about exploration I'd rather you **sign your name on the next page and pass it on** to friends or family, or donate to charities or readers in the UK or abroad.

Let's see how far this book can travel!

Write what you want!

Name, date, location and message always work.

To Granny

For reasons you'll read

"Be as I am – a reluctant enthusiast ... a part-time crusader, a half-hearted fanatic. Save the other half of yourselves and your lives for pleasure and adventure. It is not enough to fight for the land; it is even more important to enjoy it. While you can. While it's still here. So get out there and hunt and fish and mess around with your friends, ramble out yonder and explore the forests, climb the mountains, bag the peaks, run the rivers, breathe deep of that yet sweet and lucid air, sit quietly for a while and contemplate the precious stillness, the lovely, mysterious, and awesome space. Enjoy yourselves, keep your brain in your head and your head firmly attached to the body, the body active and alive, and I promise you this much; I promise you this one sweet victory over our enemies, over those desk-bound men and women with their hearts in a safe deposit box, and their eyes hypnotized by desk calculators. I promise you this: you will outlive the bastards."

Edward Abbey

Contents

PROLOGUE

When it comes to riding motorbikes, I'm an enthusiast. The open road and rush of wind is exhilarating. But I wouldn't describe myself as a motorbike enthusiast. Any explanation of motorbikes may be incorrect or ill-described in the event that you find any in the following pages. What a truly remarkable mode of transport, though!

After an array of jobs, working locally and abroad in labouring, farm work, door-to-door sales, bartending, fence erecting, and decorating, I found myself back home in Cheddar, aged twenty-one and needing funds. I had few qualifications outside of college to my name, having spent the last three years travelling for the most part. It was time to get my head down and join the working world, although this wasn't what I had envisioned. I applied everywhere in Bristol. Pubs, banks, mortgage advisers ... I fell onto the welcome mat of a high-end FTSE-listed recruitment company.

This trip and change in life motivation came about because of that job.

Truth be told, I understood little of what the job entailed at the time. I went along for the ride and soon found myself caught up in it all.

After the final interview, their ultimate concern was that I wouldn't fit into the office as, in their words, I had more of a "loner profile". I was travelling on my own the years prior, so it was partially true, but I convinced them otherwise. I'd blagged my way through the interviews with anecdotes of hard work abroad and tales of the people I met. I was hired in one of my two rotation charity-shop shirts and slip-on school shoes. And so started the suit-and-tie dissent. (For weddings, funerals and formal occasions, granted, you crack on. But sat at a desk all day? Come on, give it a rest.)

It wasn't your typical dusty office environment with dreary photocopiers, beige walls and equally oatmeal-flavoured colleagues blending into the backdrop. There were "new deal" water slides across the office floor, bicycle rides down the road wearing nothing but underwear, excessive company bar tabs, obnoxious office nights out, after-hours rail rides in the boardroom and two-litre milk showers on the zebra crossing, with staff whistling and chanting out the windows: "First deal! Whoop whoop!" It was like *The Wolf of Wall Street*, but we were more like *The Pugs of Hedge Lane*.

If you survived your first twelve months, you were doing well. It was a high-turnover job that people fall into and most fall out of, either by trying to reclaim their soul and mental health, or because they're proper shit at spinning multiple plates at a pointlessly high pace to reach the targets set by those that make all of the money your hard work brings in.

You might have done very well out of the "in it for yourself" system, planning to buy your way out, flexing your social values. Though you can't doubt it can be a cruel place for those who slip through the gaps.

Not everyone I met in the industry was a soulless shark, not by any stretch, but there was that general stigma. There are those that have the right selfless values at heart, who do very well at milking the capitalist environment. They can survive the toxic mental reverberations but fall into the influencing trap of an earn, spend, earn, spend mentality that encourages climbing the financial ladder to reach a position that will be the ticket to happiness and give you the image you think you need, regardless of the hierarchy and self-imposed stress that system causes. To reach the "top" is, more often than not, at the expense of others.

The realisation that I'd been lynched hit me square in the face as I purchased a super durability, no ironing needed, tightly woven yet breathable, finest two-fold cotton shirt from Cabot Circus. By now I'd been in the business for a couple of years. I was doing well and progressing quickly, having broken company promotion records, all the while passing shit down the ladder as quickly as it came – some call this delegation, but I found it's a power trip. I was walking out of the shop, having bought the shirt, when I had the resounding thought: *What has happened to me?*

I started thinking about the several years travelling in the logbook prior to working there, living on a budget with basic gear. I hitchhiked town to town with a skateboard and tent, from Adelaide to Melbourne, then up to Sydney. I was chased out of a Thai bungalow resort with a crossbow. I taught windsurfing in Maine, USA. I arrived by bus in Manhattan, New York, and flashed a borrowed, expired ID card in a bar. Once inside, I successfully made friends with a wedding party and a bloke offered his couch if I bought him a hot dog and promised not to murder him. The following year I owned a 1986 Toyota Landcruiser that ran on LPG Gas, moving from beach to beach around Australia. I worked the fence line on cattle stations and mine sites. I humped bananas and lived in a campsite for two months, exchanging fruits with other farm workers. I was exploring and learning about communities and the varied environments they lived in. I was meeting people from all over the world in campsites, hostels and in bumfuck nowhere, learning about their traditions, habits, styles of cooking, and outlook on life. I was learning about the treatment of the environment and the impact of change over time. I wouldn't hesitate to engage in conversation with anyone. I was happy being alone, challenging nature with the basics, at a foundation level. It's a highly recommended way of finding things out about yourself that you didn't know. I didn't realise how much so, and how much more I had to find out, until I was no longer there.

I entered this job on the basis I had no money and lack of direction as to what career path might suit me best. I had decent life experience and a perspective that suggested that I was a fifty-year-old man, yet I didn't know where to search. I couldn't find an answer.

As a result, I put my head down and worked unsavoury hours, under the impression I had to work my way up this ladder, that I was helping people in the process, that it was enhancing my image. In reality it wasn't my image, and I could see others wrapped up in it as well. I was helping myself with the salary and commission that, pretending to be a reward, bribed me to forget about the fact that the organisation was more than likely not doing our collective futures any favours, while most of the rewards of that work went to distant shareholders. The money was in the wrong place! I didn't know that at the time. Don't get me wrong, I'm not preaching. I danced with the devil and wasn't helping our collective future either. Our climate is in crisis, and I placed engineers in fossil fuel and coal companies without awareness or hesitation. A deal was a deal at the time, and I didn't see past the pressure.

Before long, I was making more money than I could ever fathom, let alone at twenty-three. It consumed me. For a lifestyle I thought I needed. I splashed cash on letting loose in Bristol city centre, carelessly spending on rounds of drinks and candy. I would struggle to drag myself out of bed in the mornings. I had nightmares of my teeth falling out. I would lie awake thinking about that deal I didn't close or that was due to close. The pressure that was put on getting that contract signed, bribed with a commission percentage, was huge. I went bright red at the first sign of a mistake. (This also happens after a couple of pints, so I'm used to it now.) There were tougher targets the harder I worked.

"Well done!" they'd say.

"Where's the next deal coming from?" immediately followed.

I waited for the weekend to surround myself with friends to get charged and remove myself from the office I worked in. There were frequent midweek booze-ups encouraged by the business for the "good of the profit". If you can't handle the pace, you're out. You could still fit in if you didn't drink, but if you did, it certainly helped.

In the office, there were underlying meanings, with excessive amounts of secrets and false praise. I pictured the wire loop game as I carefully moved the metal loop with both hands along the twisted path of the electric wire. Every touch of the wire would result in a slap-in-the-face "Game Over" shock. Restart from the beginning. The thought of giving up the job and the money, of starting over, was distant and daunting. This circled my mind. I never completed the game.

It reached a point after a few years where I'd found a balance of working the bare minimum during the day, leaving at 5 p.m. and not caring about the progression; everything still felt false. I would smoke myself into oblivion as soon as I got home, to remove my mind from myself. There was little moderation.

I was going to take the steps to leave, regardless of the costs. I couldn't continue to contribute to the selfish system that leaves so many people in society behind. My sights were set on completing my unrestricted motorcycle licence at twenty-four (direct access) and putting into play an exit plan for as long as I could hack it, while availing myself of the opportunity for any training and business experience by partnering our CSR programme with Bristol charities that would help community projects and, undoubtedly, my prospects. I was going to take on Iberia by Bike: France, Spain, Portugal and Andorra (which I'd opted to miss), and I'd have A Merry Ride Round along the way.

Under the advice of my dad, an experienced Blood Biker volunteer, in preparation for my trip but also for general motorbike-riding safety knowledge, I undertook the IAM Advanced Rider course (Institute of Advanced Motorcyclists) through my local SAM group (Somerset Advanced Motorcyclists). I booked my first observation ride with the instructor and agreed to meet in a car park one afternoon. For a quick top-up of fuel before the ride, I popped into Morrisons down the road. I placed the hose nozzle back into the large slot labelled "Diesel". *Shit.* I realised my mistake.

"Daadddd, where are you? ... Please bring a hose." Something to do with the high compression ratio – more noise, more vibration – is why there aren't really any diesel engines on bikes, in case you were wondering. (A quick internet search on my part; you're welcome.) What did I say about bike facts? Apologies, that may or may not be the last one.

I straddled the tank, lips puckered over the hose. I sucked, then spluttered, to siphon the fuel concoction out. The instructor and my dad stood at the side, making all manner of thoroughly deserved mocking remarks. What a terrific start to the advanced rider course that was. I did pass the course after this journey. It's an extremely worthwhile course for any motorist on two or four wheels.

The mind and feet of a young, pent-up, reluctantly corporate-working, movement-seeking, purpose-pursuing, machine-owning man-child can wander. I found that when my feet were on a motorbike, they were able to wander further. This is a log of those travels, mistakes and findings, with recommended road names, actual people and real events. The words and experiences that follow in this journey are my own. In some instances, I share things that I've not been comfortable enough to speak about before, in the hope that if you need to, it'll encourage you to do the same.

Dive in, ride off, or step out, whichever works for you, but take the decision to discover what your meaning of happy is, which may well be outside of the standard nine-to-five (and can still include all your home comforts). The philosopher Daniel Dennett puts it this way: "The secret of happiness: Find something more important than you are and dedicate your life to it."

I'm still looking for mine, but I think I'm heading down the right path.

Yours may not be fleeing clouds and writing shit about them, but as Cheddar cheesy as it sounds, I'm prepared to join the world in my way, rather than hide in a tailored suit that doesn't fit my bulging mould. With ease, I now get up earlier than I ever had to for that job. A small but notable difference. More or less what I'm trying to say is that I have significantly less now, but really, I have so much more.

You've either found it or you haven't. If you haven't, then consider spending time with nature to figure things out. If you're one of the eighty-five per cent of people that don't like their jobs,[1] ask yourself why that is and try to do something about it.

You'll know.

---

1   A global poll conducted by Gallup in 2017 has uncovered that out of the world's one billion full-time workers, only 15% of people are engaged at work.

Lost items list

2 plastic camping cups

1 notebook

4 pens

a red pottery mug

a wooden spoon

dignity on occasions

a spare set of keys for pannier boxes, padlock & mesh
    locking

2 ear-piercing studs

tent & poles

marbles

cards

Final statistics

roughly 9,999 kilometres (km)/6213 miles

65 days

1 Honda Shadow VT750 motorbike – "the Shadow"

4 tyres & 1 bike service

1 water-damaged passport

3 foot pegs

2 sleeping bags & 1 blanket

a number of bottles of red wine

total money spent inc. fuel, not inc. week holiday
    with Princess Tasha and the Chicas = averaged
    about £35 per day including fuel & the occasional
    accommodation

The following text will have distances measured in kilometres (km) as the journey was through Europe. For the imperial minds: this simple calculation has helped my poor arithmetic when converting to miles. (I won't be offended if you skip to Chapter 1.)

1 mile = 1.6 km

1 km = 0.62 miles

To work out a close enough calculation for miles from kilometres in your head, see below:

- Divide total km by 2
- Divide total km by 10
- Add both answers together to get your *near enough* miles as that's all we ever really need

- 300 km ÷ 2 = 150
- 300 km ÷ 10 = 30
- 150 + 30 = 180 miles (roughly – exact answer is 186.41)

Try the following. You'll find the answer at the end of the book:

- 500 km ÷ 2 =
- 500 km ÷ 10 =
- ___ + ___ = miles

BAY OF BISCAY

BILBAO

NAZARE
WAVE

PORTO

MINHO
CANTABRIAN
MOUNTAINS

DOURO

IBS

PORTUGAL

MADRID

TAGUS
CENTRAL
SIERRA RAL

GUADIANA

SPAIN

LISBON

GUADALQUIVIR

BAE
SYSTEM

SEVILLE

ALBO

BENAGIL CAVES

MOROCCO

1
FOR GRANNY

"Me voy por la mañana" in Spanish translates as "I leave in the morning", which was the first phrase I'd learnt. To be used if caught by authorities trying to camp somewhere for free.

At my grandmother's ninetieth birthday, family and friends from far and wide gathered to celebrate. Granny to me, Auntie

Bet to others, Betty Chalkley by name, known by many and disliked by none. A published author (*Betty's Book of Family Tales*), an accomplished hang-glider (at eighty years of age!), a Coronavirus survivor at ninety-two, a great-granny, the oldest of her siblings and as such the link between our family's past and present. Everyone looks up to her, yet she looks down on no one. An honourable heroine, and to be frank, an absolute legend. The story doesn't start here, but this is where we'll begin.

The next weekend I was at the pub with friends when the text message came. The ferry had been brought forward by eight hours due to bad weather, causing an abrupt end to a Sunday session superseded by frantic packing. I was in good spirits ahead of the due departure. The Rugby World Cup '19 was already in full swing and on the telly was Wales v Georgia (43–14 FT).

I departed from Cheddar Gorge that Monday morning, wind in my ears and fuel in the tank. Within ten minutes I made a discovery, which was how ill prepared for the weather I was. For the water had sneakily seeped its way through my so-called waterproof overtrousers and into my already heavy Kevlar motorbike jeans. My slip-on motorbike boots sloshed like a reservoir. I had a wetter crotch than Sunday night of Glastonbury Festival and no clue what navigating Salisbury would be like on a bike in the rain. Thirty minutes of twat laps trying to find parking when wet, cold and hungry was not the envisioned start. The first stop was an outdoor shop selling hiking gaiters, in an attempt to stop the waterfall gushing in through the top of my boots. The lightweight camping chair was an additional pleasure purchase. I felt like royalty each night, sat on my throne, as it slotted like an architectural dream into the tent porch on rainy days.

On to the M27 I hit the worst combination of rain, fog and southern-coast commuters I've experienced in the UK to this day. As the traffic slowed, the smug opportunity to push on through arose, leaving motorists behind frustrated but dry at least.

So followed the arrival of the ferry as I stood with other soggy motorcyclists in the queue. Bikes were ratchet-strapped in the vehicle hold as I removed the clothing bags required before heading up to find my cabin.

The ferry bar was a busy watering hole around 11.30 p.m., ahead of the 12.05 a.m. departure. All the ark-enclosed creatures came down for a drink. Retired motorhome elephants sipped their vino tinto, and hyenas on tour over-ordered at last orders, as the weather conditions made for increasingly tricky walking, drinking and smoking. Smokers ignored the bold "Deck Closed" sign to have a cheeky cig in the thick of the blotchy sky outside, before the ferry tucked in for the night and sailed across the ocean, absorbed in the dark cloud blanket of the night as it rose and fell with every bad-weather wave.

As we rolled into Tuesday, a pattern of eating, drinking, sleeping then repeating took up the entire day. Enduring some unwanted uneasiness and unexpected napping, I spent most of the day in my room, my musty damp jeans drying, with the occasional venture out to eat. The boat danced like the boat that rocked, but in place of the smooth Sixties soundtrack was a cacophony of chatter, glasses, and speaker announcements.

Everyone's partial to a bit of people watching. Ferry people watching is next level. The sheer contrast between the elegant staff as they glide like *Dancing on Ice* professionals through the bar, carrying trays piled high with plates and drinks towering above their heads, and the recently boarded customers making their way down corridors like fawns freshly out of their deer mother's womb taking their first steps. I recalled watching an inelegant swan on icy flooded fields down on the Somerset Levels similarly losing their dignity until reaching the safety of water. Safety of the bar, in this case.

Later, as I bounded down to the restaurant for dinner, I encountered a confused elderly lady in the café section. She clamped the handrail, nearly ripping it off. I observed her mouth the word "butter", for her otherwise dry bread roll. Knowing where the butter lived, and treading carefully, I approached and offered to help the senior damsel in distress. When travelling alone, it's that time for observation that is cherished. It's those small encounters and interactions that keep you guessing. It can be a lonely place at times, but it's yours to action. I would like to affirm that it's not just elderly interactions I seek out. You filthy animals. Although what follows doesn't help my case.

Planting my feet on the swaying ship to counterbalance the motion, we swayed back and forth.

I must take my opportunity between the waves.

"I believe the butter is over there," I said, offering assistance.

Mumbling the word "there", I cast out my hand to offer a physical direction. At that precise moment, the ship threw a wobbly, an iceberg-like shift in direction. My gesture reared off course, thrusting a backhand into her right bosom. The red face of embarrassment arrived at the point of realisation that I was not pointing at the butter but slapping her breast. Unsurprisingly she shrieked in shock. What followed was an unfamiliar state. I racked my brains on how to handle the situation, almost echoing her scream. No amount of conflict resolution and sales training was going to get me out of this unscathed.

I apologised profusely, almost on the verge of nervous laughter, and swiftly exited via the gift shop towards the restaurant, leaving her clinging to the rail with her still dry bread roll.

We'll both be telling that story at book club for years to come.

2
ON MY MERRY WAY

Having just about dried my boots, jeans and gloves in the cabin, we docked in Bilbao port. The night had been rough and, regardless of the nightcaps, I'd struggled to sleep. It was 8 a.m. with the whole day ahead. I'd planned to wander around Bilbao and stay for the first night, but I was too excited to get on the road. I rode off in any direction the road went, with a rough plan inland to Sabiñánigo, a town at the base of the Pyrenees, halfway between the Bay of Biscay and the Mediterranean.

Prepay fuel. *What is this all about?* You have to guess the amount of fuel you need, pay for it, then fill up. Unsure of the process, wanting to ensure that I got a full tank, I requested €15. The tank clicked out at €7. *What am I supposed to do now?* I went back inside and joined a queue six people deep. I waited for what felt like a lifetime and no one had moved, so I turned on my heels and escaped. Desperate to get on the road but also a little embarrassed to return to the service desk meant I didn't hang around to claim my money back. *I wonder what the expiry date on the receipt is.*

My first experience with a GoPro camera ensued. After the fuel station, I pulled over to fix it to my helmet. Why I recorded half an hour of the least interesting roads of the trip I don't know, as I sat in traffic for the most part. However, at roughly twenty-four minutes, thirteen seconds, I had an encounter, caught on the footage:

I turn off the main road away from traffic to look for somewhere safe and convenient to pull over for a self-regroup. I've been riding for an hour or so without breakfast, and my stomach is having a heated conversation with my brain. The chosen road very quickly starts heading up a steep hill which soon narrows and loses quality. It's tarmac that hasn't been properly rolled, like small consecutive speed bumps, and I'm rattling on the bike, as my arse leaves the seat over each one. Up ahead there's a car parked in a lay-by, which gives me good enough reason to attempt a turn. I'm hungry making this decision. I know this isn't the best place to turn but I've committed. I've noticed that a car has pursued us close behind since turning off the main road. In mid-manoeuvre the car pulls up right next to my front wheel, blocking my turn, and manually winds down the window of a rustic Renault. I'm still focusing on not falling over down the hill, a bit frustrated at this driver cutting me up.

> *A frowning señora addresses me in Spanish.*
> *Señora: "Hola."* (Hello.)
> *J (me): "Hola."* (Hello.)
> *S: "Eres el dueño del coche?"* (Are you the owner of this car?)
> *J: "Pardon?"* (Pardon?)
> *S: "Es dueño de este coche?"* (Do you own this car?)
> *I was thinking this Spanish I've learnt isn't coming to much use as I understand nothing, and then part mutter in French.*
> *J: "Um ... no es parle en español ... [pause] Pardon?"* (Um ... I don't speak Spanish ... Pardon?)
> *S: "Eres el dueño del coche?"* (Are you the owner of this car?)
> *J: [silence]*
> *S: "Este coche es tuyo?"* (Is this car yours?)
> *J: "Me?"* (Me?)
> *S: "Sí."* (Yes.)
> *J: "Para mí?"* (For me?)

Speaking over the sound of the engine I struggle to hear, let alone understand what is going on. I turn off the engine. There is a long pause as she shakes her head at me. I can feel myself turning red under my helmet.

S: *[louder this time, with pointing]* *"Este coche, es tuyo?"* (This car, is yours?)

J: *[shaking my head]* *"I don't know."*

S: *"Es porque lleva aquí mucho tiempo, y cuando vi la matrícula extranjera pensé que era tuyo."* (It is because it has been here for a long time, and when I saw the foreign registration, I thought it was yours.)

J: *[silence]*

Trying not to be rude, I was thinking that if I didn't understand her earlier questions, how was I going to understand that.

S: *"No me entiendes?"* (Don't you understand me?)

Clearly not.

J: *[shaking my head, repeating what she said]* *"No me entiendes."* (You don't understand me.)

S: *"Qué eres? Francés o qué?"* (What are you? French or what?)

J: *"Inglés."* (English.)

S: *"Inglés ... ah! [a wave of the hand] Lleva aquí mucho, mucho tiempo, y no sabemos de quién es."* (English ... ah! It's spent a long time here, a long time, and we don't know whose it is.)

J: *"Okay, sí, gracias."* (Okay, yes, thank you.)

She gives up and drives off with a perfect hill start, although I suspect it's an automatic. My Spanish is terrible!

Shortly after my first Spanish interaction, feeling flustered and like I'd not got very far, I needed coffee and food. I pulled into an urban park for a break. I took out my lightweight gas cooker and percolator from the back panniers and brewed a coffee to have with a bread roll and butter I'd swiped from the ferry.

This was the first moment on Spanish soil that it sank in: *I'm on my own from now on, and I don't have a clue what I'm doing.*

The remainder of the day was filled with remarkable sights. Jagged ruins capped hillsides, and streams of ploughed, earthy brown fields ran into waxy green treetops, with sandy castles appearing on the horizon. Pure smiles all day. I bought my supplies (a daily intake of bread, chorizo, cheese and fruit) from a local Spanish supermarket called Lidl, realised I should have found an actual local market to support, then headed on to a succession of dusty inland towns. Rarely did I see anyone on the streets or a café open.

It was an absolutely amazing first day that set up the rest of the trip. I'd travelled 450 km without a single motorway section touched, a rule I'd decided I should stick to throughout the trip.

As 4 p.m. approached, I found a campsite online that I deemed a suitable stay: Camping Luesia. Remote and basic.

Perfect. The turn into there off the A-1202 was a stony dirt track, with the campsite signposted 10 km further along it. My bike was a Honda Shadow – similar to a Harley Davidson but supposedly more reliable, shaft drive, shiny, low to the ground, designed for straight open roads and comfort. Not for a stony, dusty, hilly, off-the-beaten-track road. I embarked down it at an almost crawling pace. Phone signal had been long gone.

The campsite was closed, with nothing but padlocked gates. Mentally exhausted and hungry, I honked the horn several times with no response. The surrounding forest was ideal for wild camping, but I'd eaten my earlier supplies and only an apple remained. I was ready to retreat to dinner, a shower and bed, but without dinner, this wasn't deemed much of an option. I saw no other way but to turn around, crawl back down the track and continue onwards.

At the nearest town of Luesia, a picturesque municipality surrounded by valleys and voluptuous views across the dirt, I found a bar to rest. The upstairs bar was empty of punters, but a type of *Top of the Pops* played on the TV. No food served until 9 p.m. *I'm sorry, what?* With a few hours to wait I ordered an espresso, then another, then a small beer. I opted to call campsites in the area, of which there were two within a forty-five-minute ride. One of the local men in the bar overheard my struggling phone conversation and, in English, pointed me in the right direction – thankfully, as I couldn't make head or tail of the call. I had to bank on it being open.

This section of the ride was incredible. Long winding corners with sharp-ending sides that you dare not go over. It wouldn't have been the death of me if I had, but best avoided.

The road sat on top of flowing sand dunes that carved their way through the landscape. I could see the next two towns ahead perched on the hills, the church almost always being the closest building to the sky. Moss the colour of emeralds topped the dunes, and dark branches that could have been shadows stuck out in all directions.

I arrived at Camping Bolaso near Sadaba, exhausted and still with nothing for dinner. Luckily, the camp shop came to my rescue. Jarred lentejas (lentils) and pitted olives, leftover festering Philly cheese and a giant bag of plain crisps, all washed down with a large screw-top beer and served with free entertainment: a bloke washing his dog's feet in the shared bathroom sink while smoking a spliff the size of a Cuban cigar.

Sat outside the tent on my throne, I felt a sharp twinge in my pants. An ant had circumnavigated its way to the inside of my pants. Without hesitation I threw serious dance moves on removal, spraying sandy soil around in all directions. To my horror, the ground was infested below my tent as ants scrambled over one another to get first dibs on dinner – me. In a hop, skip and jump, avoiding ants like a scene out of *Indiana Jones*, up came the tent pegs and out came the poles to move to a less congested area.

A short lie-in followed the next morning, with nowhere urgent to be yet. The only other camper, a cyclist, was gone by the time I got out of the shower. After careful deliberation post-packing up – on average it took between one and two hours from getting up to having everything on the back of the Shadow – I decided to break my rule set the day before and it was bloody brilliant for the most part. I took the motorway towards Sabiñánigo where I was completely outpowered by some 1200000000 cc BMW bikes that roared past my 750 cc V-Twin. After an hour twenty on the road, it rose into a winding nervous system entwined with the mountainous flesh and carved artery tunnels that allowed the flow of traffic. The prequel to the Pyrenees. A delicious morsel.

I stopped for a coffee, small beer and tapas lunch in Sabiñánigo after passing a large collective of bikers, maybe thirty-odd, of all shapes and sizes. I sat chatting with two French off-road bikers laden with gear, including spare tyres hanging off the back, who had crossed the border for a few days. What a place to have easy access to.

Next up was north into the thick of the Pyrenees range on the N-330a, passing Formigal. I missed the England v USA (45–7 FT) rugby game in the process. Rarely do I not think about a rugby match if I know it's on, and this was one of those times. But at the time of note writing, I wrote "best road I have driven", and it's still up there.

An ongoing habit is to compare places seen to Cheddar Gorge, which is a natural wonder in itself. "It ain't no Cheddar Gorge though, is it, boys?" said in the most yokel accent one can muster. It crossed my mind again as I approached the foothills of the Pyrenees. I stopped to sort out the GoPro on my helmet. The footage certainly revealed some of my poor road riding lines, but also showed the scale of the remarkable scenery on either side. A wise piece of advice I've always remembered, from driving quad bikes in the Welsh hills, was to stop to look at the view instead of looking whilst driving. Otherwise, the view gets a lot closer than you'd like as you topple off the edge.

High-rise rock faces appeared following each bend. Layered levels of shaded grey met crystal blue skies overhead before falling sharply into scattered collections of buildings in the valley below, where equally lucid water flowed around them.

I scraped the low footrest on the acute corners more times than not on this section, too excited, not considering the bike's lack of ability to take on corners. I quickly learnt the flick of the left hand to regular oncoming bikers; in the UK a nod of the head is more common, considering your offside hand is on the throttle and should stay there. My helmet's visor was overcome with an assortment of bugs, much like a fly lolly. They refused to shift with the force of the wind, therefore I took regular stops to wipe and stretch. I welcomed the breaks to enjoy the surrounding environment from the safety of being stationary. At one of the highest points on the route, just after Formigal, I took a longer stop to soak in the view and take a few pictures. Not yet snow-capped, the embodied natural palette of the mountain peaks and shadows from the clouds transcended visual boundaries as I stood in silence.

I crossed into France on a Tour de France route and camped at Laruns for the night. After three unsuccessful attempts, I found a campsite that wasn't closed. (There were some misleading opening times online.) It was certainly tiresome limiting yourself to campsites found on the day, as extra riding and searching was required. Booking in advance would alleviate this task. However, once successful, when your tent is up and the pot is simmering with the chickpeas and chorizo bought from the shop earlier, and you're a couple of glasses of red down, it makes it oh-so sweeter to sit back in the tent porch on your throne. No ants this time, but plenty of wet sand to dirty everything that lay on it and a sky lit fabulously bright by the stars. I didn't need the torch to see what a mess I'd really made; it was a bit late for shoes off at the door.

notes

- antimosquito spray in abundance needed after multiple forehead bites

3
JIMMY

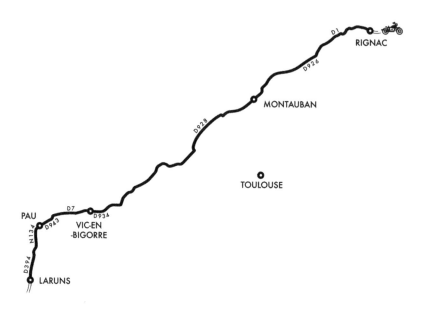

The following morning, after a coffee had been brewed and a pain au chocolat devoured, I was packed up and ready to take on France. It was cold enough to freeze the balls off a brass monkey. The roads were at a high enough altitude to notice, and they offered silky speed. I was thermalled up to the max, heading straight north to Pau. I'd completely misjudged the weather with the lack of gear I had available to use. Quaint little French villages would appear after stretches of woodland and fenced farmland as I weaved my way around the scenic course. A church on a roundabout got a few laps and a photo. It occurred to me that crossing the roundabout to get to a service would be significantly easier than trying to navigate the Arc de Triomphe through kamikaze traffic. No underground walkway required for this picturesque building.

Late for lunch, I reached Vic-en-Bigorre. Hunger had hit me long before my arrival but there had been no food-stop options except cornfields. Once again, hunger impacted my decision-making as I scouted for somewhere to park. Thus followed a park-off. An elderly lady and I locked eyes, her Peugeot poised, the Shadow stationary on the cusp of launch. The onlookers sat outside a café in search of entertainment on the dry but cloudy early afternoon were lucky today. It was her right of way.

After parking elsewhere, I sat down in a small café-bar and ordered an espresso. The food menu teased me as it hung on the wall. It was one of those exciting menus with perfect pictures of the dishes on offer. I licked my lips. I made eye contact with the waiter.

"No food," he said.

My belly replied. The second eye-staring contest I'd lost in quick succession. I shot the coffee and settled on pizza bread from the next-door bakery, which filled the sides but wasn't the toastie and chips I'd envisioned when I sat down.

On I rode. A group of local teenagers on their motos honked their horns as I passed some charming gardens split by a stream.

Above Toulouse I travelled in the rough direction of Rodez, avoiding the main roads where possible. Close encounters on tight country bends, meeting tractors cutting corners, were a regular occurrence. A familiar one back home as well! I made a coffee and cigarette stop around late afternoon – maybe it was at Montauban, but I'd lost my way so I'm not one hundred per cent sure on this. There, I used online maps to make a rough estimate of time and available campsites within my self-imposed limit left for the day. Rignac was the goal, yet I was unaware of what awaited us there.

I made two pit stops after Montauban. The first was to pick up antimosquito spray from a glowing green cross (a pharmacy, not an Irish bar), where I also picked up a speeding ticket for my troubles which was posted to my mum's back home. I'd promised I'd ride safe and slow. Worth paying if I was to ride France again. The second stop was at a roadside bar for a small beer and an espresso (a frequent rocket-fuel combination). The barman, a jolly, well-padded fellow – in character and stature – was intrigued by my journey. In a jiffy, upon request, my road map was sprawled across the bar. Using hand gestures and the odd French word, I explained to him (it was at this point I related him to Obelix, from *Asterix)* where I'd come from in recent days. His rounded, rosy-red face responded with "Because of Brexit!" at the top of his voice, assuming that's why I'd done the distance in such a short time. "Lots to see before you leave," he added. The handful of thick accents sitting at the bar were all laughing profusely. I took it well by laughing with them, red-faced, almost feeling the need to apologise. I've had the discussion with a friend that for someone who lived permanently outside of their home country during Brexit, jokes like that were likely frequent and would soon become tiresome; the kind of remarks that us Brits wouldn't think twice about making, completely unaware of their impact.

The attention-seeking resident ginger cat had wandered outside and started snooping around my motorbike. Two of the local customers I'd just been laughing with took an interest as well. At first glance, it looked as though the cat had leapt up and perched on the back seat, but the cat was nowhere to be seen. Jimmy Juggler sat proudly on the bike, head high, top lip protruding and gangly arms securing my luggage. It was Jimmy who the Frenchmen were interested in.

By way of introduction, Jimmy is my puppet monkey. A puppet monkey? I hear you ask. He makes up the "we" in this story.

Jimmy was a prominent figure growing up. My uncle sold the puppet monkeys down the markets. There was Billy Baboon, Olly Orangutan, Matty Monkey and Gary Gorilla, who all came to life with a bit of imagination and an effective seller. Obviously Granny was the best. Her front room was scattered with sewing machines and plastered with felt and stuffing as we made our own monkey versions.

On the day I left, Jimmy caught my eye, hanging from the curtain rail in my bedroom. On the spur of the moment, I extended the invitation to him and took the silence as a "yes". For the sole reason that it would be rather amusing to have a monkey sitting on the back of a motorbike, safeguarding my belongings, his head bobbing around with the flow of the wind. Who in their right mind would steal a bike of its luggage under the nose of a cute, cuddly toy monkey? This was my theory, anyway.

Although I enjoy solo travel and the challenges it throws at you, no one wants to be completely alone. I thought he would make me more approachable outside of the rambunctious motorbike, black visor helmet and matching leather jacket. Jimmy has made many appearances at Glastonbury Festival, always drawing attention with his curly locks and Mr Tickle-like arms. He became a familiar talisman year on year in our group, helping to navigate through the large crowds – "Follow the monkey!" – and avoid getting separated. Ravers passing by would usually stroke him or ask for a cuddle. As soon as he woke up and came to life, it would go one of two ways: true love or sheer terror. He was a successful, innocent-looking mule, with a secret zip pocket in his back for the festival's concoction of juggling balls.

I arrived in Rignac, not far from Rodez, almost dozing off at the sight of the sleepy town. The second most expensive campsite of the entire trip at €17. And the emptiest! I was given use of a stationary mobile homes for the shower and bathroom as the main facility was closed for the season. I contemplated taking the bed to sleep in as I was the only camper in the village, but thought better of it and set up my tent.

After setting up camp, I wandered into the centre to find dinner and a beverage. I found the only place open on a Friday night and entered with a sceptical smile. It turned out to be a superb family-run bar and restaurant named Le Patio. After ten small beers and an additional free one, I learnt that they were motorbike enthusiasts and also owned a Honda Shadow!

I couldn't keep up with the bike chat therefore quickly steered it to a broken yet enjoyable conversation with the locals about football, why my face went red when drinking alcohol, how rosé wine is better than beer for the belly, and some advice on roads to ride in the local area. I ended up back in my mobile home, smoking a large cigar and sending drunken Snapchats to mates back home. None of which I could recall in the morning when reading their replies.

4
CHERRY BLOSSOMS

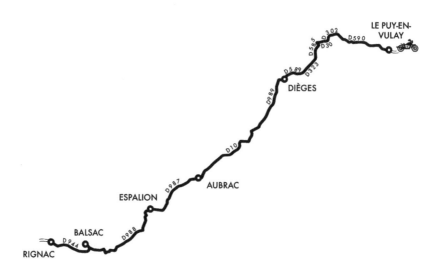

Yet again another cold start but it had not yet affected my spirits. It was a Saturday, rugby match day. I donned my Winscombe RFC shirt and Jimmy waved his Combe towel. I'd usually be playing fly half, but on this occasion I found another bench on which to eat my cheese and chorizo sarnie and watch the second half of the Ireland v Japan (12–19 FT) game on my phone. Japan yet again made history as they won in what was the biggest rugby upset since they beat South Africa in the 2015 World Cup. I was left gobsmacked in the park, jumping around in excitement, wanting someone other than Jimmy to share the moment with, but no passers-by put up their hand to my hanging high five. Well done to the brave Cherry Blossoms!

I had left Rignac on the D994 towards Rodez, then veered off to detour through Balsac because it had a great name. Many more back roads later, I joined the D988 just before Espalion to sit down for the game. Afterwards, fully fed and flustered, I hit the highland region of the Massif Central on the D987. I considered swinging by Condom-d'Aubrac but I'd had enough phallic place names for the day.

I pulled over and switched the engine off to allow local farmers and their bells to herd cows down the road. It seemed to be a family occasion and a chance for chatter. Jimmy gazed at the larger beasts, but thankfully they took no interest in him.

The walking region of Parc naturel régional de l'Aubrac came into view. High up and covered in lying mist, it hovered motionless, like an intricately knitted cobweb that could not be wiped away. Hillsides in the shade to the north had a halo cloud spanning the entire landscape. There were, of course, power lines resting in the foreground, forever present. I opted to go deeper into the natural park. "Not Giving In" by Rudimental came on through the headphones from an old playlist I'd put on. Memories of leaving college in the summer of '12 poured through. I listened to this song blaring out of the car stereo at many parties that year. *I really need to update my playlists.*

I entered the village of Aubrac, whose name also applies to the surrounding countryside, to be greeted by dreary grey stone buildings and equally grey people moseying around, either arriving or leaving for walks. It was necessary to put on another layer to combat the cold. I could see why the outside of the buildings lacked character – although this was part of its interesting nature – as it was frightfully cold, no one wanted to spend too long outside. I headed into one of the two cafés, Jimmy begrudgingly left to guard the bike. What a contrast! The inside was marvellous. My jacket was off before the large door closed. A fire roared at the end of the room, catching my gaze. I thought I heard it crackle as I walked in. A gold-lettered plaque declaring the village name hung above it, glistening. The place was packed with people and atmosphere, seemingly unchanged since it first opened. Fromage soup warmed the cockles but was cheesier than I could handle, and I'm from Cheddar! That said, the French would claim our beloved local cheese to be mild and boring. I won't engage in that argument.

Whilst the village of Aubrac had an old-age appeal, the surrounding views were as scenic as they come. Even in the cloud and cold, it emitted a sense of calming collectiveness with the play of light off the shimmering trees that seemed incandescent. The road that headed out of the natural park imitated the turns of a roller coaster, with thick treelines either side and small barbed wire fence lines, allowing obnoxious full-throttle riding.

Some hours later, the harsh air still rife, I arrived in Le Puy-en-Velay after a lovely scenic ride. It has to be up there as one of the easiest cities to navigate. The two reference-point landmarks floating high above the city mean you know where you are in relation to where you need to be. The Saint-Michel d'Aiguilhe chapel from the tenth century perches on volcanic rock, as does the statue of Notre-Dame de France built in 1860. Pure beacons in the landscape. I'd have liked to have climbed them both, but due to the time of week and meagre money I had, I managed neither.

The real star of the show arose at night-time, and by complete good fortune I was there to witness the illumination show. It only runs from July to the end of September, and I caught the final night. Vast arrays of colours combined with melodies in moving pictures kept the audience captivated in silence. The tints were thrown around and ricocheted off the features of the historical buildings, incorporating them by design into the stories told. The show illustrated on the twelfth-century Romanesque Notre-Dame Cathedral was the highlight for me. Incredible pieces of artwork and technical brilliance. I highly recommend this place to visit and, if possible, to see the show too. Between each illuminated production you are able to wander the cobbled streets free of charge.

I'd have been inclined to stay another day in the city campsite, but treading in dog shite twice – one of which was right outside the door of my tent – drove me to leave. Regardless, Le Puy is on the list of places to revisit.

notes

- a roach-sized card is missing from 28 Sep in my notebook – I can't comment on what day this took place

- a decent freestyle pizza show from the engaging staff at Pizzeria Le Golden, followed by a sublime pizza

5
NOT SO EASY LIKE SUNDAY MORNING

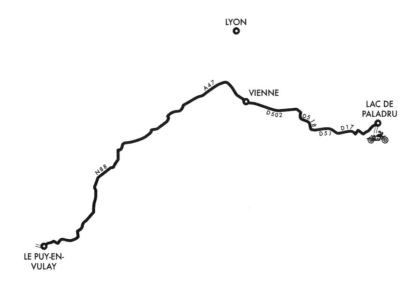

The last Sunday of the month but my first in France. Unbeknown to myself, there were few fuel stations open on the day of rest and the ones left were machine operated. Not usually a problem; however, Mastercard wasn't working with any of them and I had no Visa. I rode through neighbouring towns twice. At the fifth rural fuel station, anxious I might not reach the next one, I stopped and waited fifteen minutes until a car approached. I asked if I could give him cash if he bought my fuel on his card. The shiny Mercedes glistening in the sun and the large watch face shoved into mine were abundant signs of his wealth, so I thought it would be no issue. He looked at me. He looked at Jimmy waiting by the pump – Jimmy always waited patiently. He looked at me again. The scrunch of his nose spoke before I heard any words: "It is not possible."

"Why?" I asked. He clearly could afford it on his card. Maybe he doesn't use cash.

"I work in a bank. My fuel goes on my company card."

Of course it does, banker wanker.

The second car arrived a few minutes later. The banker was gone. An old beat-up people carrier pulled up to the pump. Mother and Father sat in the front, toddler in the back. I asked the same question. They were happy to help after I pleaded with Puss in Boots's eyes. Jimmy sparked curiosity from their rear seat; little hands spread wide on the glass as eyes peered through in between. The contrast between the family and the banker couldn't have been more apparent. I gave them the extra change I had for their troubles and made my merry motorway to Lac de Paladru (Lake Paladru), between Chambéry and Grenoble. I took the fast N88, A47 then A7 through a picturesque Vienne, just in case of persisting petrol problems, before peeling off south-east to my destination.

The next couple of days were spent relaxing on the lake shore. Monday was a national day of mourning to honour the late French president Jacques Chirac, who'd died a few days earlier, so flags were at half mast and nothing was open. I'd driven this way to catch up with Patrice, a talented engineer with a vast wine collection, who I'd met through my previous office job. We'd discovered we had a relatively mutual outlook on life, politics and motorbikes. Naturally we got on well from the first business lunch and kept in contact through multiple contracts.

(N.B. I still keep an eye out for jobs for him. If you're looking for an experienced Project Manager/Engineer, let me know and I'll charge you some ridiculous commission for the introduction ... He knows.)

Before dinner with Patrice and Katherine at their place that night, I spent the day on the lake's beach. A sight for sore eyes as I watched Scotland v Samoa (34–0 FT) on my phone: a woman bathed near the shores for the lens whilst a man stood behind the camera on a stepladder, to cover all the angles. Supposedly a common scene for the lakeside mountain views. Obviously, like any human being in a relationship, I dared not survey the scene. I ignored it, diverting my gaze out across the lake. I was more in shock than anything else. It was cringey and peculiar to witness. I instantly didn't like the potbellied man perched on the ladder. I wasn't sure why. *Magazine front covers must come from somewhere, I suppose.*

I had a realisation that I'd be very interested in owning a back garden abreast a lake. A combination of a café, campsite, windsurfing, events and good times. Now, I'm no lake expert but I have experienced lakes in Maine, USA, Lago de Garda in Italy, and now in France – and obviously Cheddar Reservoir gets another mention. *I am still deciding where this venture might be.*

notes

- Patrice is no longer on the market
- many thanks, Patrice and Katherine, for your hospitality, great advice and a lovely drop of vino

6
SKINNY-DIPPING

Entering Grenoble from the north revealed an attractive valley plunge as the city emerged, wedged between long, sloping, mountainous walls at the foot of the French Alps. The scenery was spectacular, but it was trumped by the stench of trapped pollution. I continued south without stopping.

The most efficient way to ride in France is on the toll roads. I avoided these at all costs. Arriving at toll gates is up there as one of my least favourite activities in foreign countries; something always goes wrong. However, in France, more so than other countries, they really rub it in if you don't use them by placing the non-toll roads (D) right next to the toll roads (A, usually), but with a much slower speed limit. You can see and hear vehicles as they roar past, taunting you.

The D1075 got interesting as I passed Monestier-de-Clermont. Those who know their history, geography or driving roads will be thinking of the Route Napoléon from Golfe-Juan on the Côte d'Azur to Grenoble, which is marked at intervals by statues of eagles. I'd made the decision to opt for the westerly roads towards Spain, which meant I didn't gaze upon the tourist eagle signage. No regrets as it was still a magnificent ride.

Turning right at Serres I came onto the D994 before the D94 – 17.5 km of greatness, Patrice had called it. He was right. The gloves were off. I set up my GoPro and waved to a couple hitchhiking; they'd put up their thumbs nonetheless in amusement.

The usual procedure began by looking for an open campsite, and again it was the fourth one where I found success. An olive farm, perched high on a hill overlooking the town of Nyons, surrounded by overhanging trees casting all manner of shadows. I treated myself to a sausage sandwich for dinner, with mustard sachets from the ferry and a sunset on the opposing hillside. Due to the stillness of the evening, I nonchalantly put up my tent on the tough ground. No guy ropes.

It's 12.40 a.m. I've been asleep for a couple of hours. I wake to a loud bang and check the time. It takes a few groggy moments to come round to the puddle of water down the side of the tent and the pounding of rain outside. Opening the inner tent, I'm greeted with a collapsed porch and sodden gear. The ground is dirt so this has splattered over everything it can reach. Quickly my raincoat goes on, and I make my way outside into the storm. The flashes of lightning are frequent and the sound of thunder follows. From a dry shelter it would be a hell of a show. Pegs in hand, I make my way to each necessary rope but I can't get the darn things in the ground. Not for the life of me. I scout the area for large rocks instead. By this point my trousers are soaked. Luckily, a collection of rocks piled around the corner comes to the rescue. I disturb a scorpion who's sheltering under one of the rocks, which makes me jump and almost lose my footing. It finds another, which I leave alone. An age later, rocks in place, the tent is taut and stable, the towel is down, clothes are off and I'm lying on my back, still rather soggy. Begging for a good sleep, I nod off, dreaming for the morning to be dry.

Fortunately it was a crisp day. A chance to hang everything out and to explore the local region with no luggage, just Jimmy on the back. A French café on the square in Nyons was open for the France v USA (33–9 FT) clash on their large TV. I sat across the car park in view of Jimmy minding the bike as he enjoyed attracting attention from walkers-by.

I made my winding way up to Bourdeaux, a small village an hour north of Nyons, embedded in the mountain scenery. My older brother and family – Kit, Esme and son, Rudy – had been there some weeks earlier visiting friends who had bought a place on the neighbouring hillside. Friends of family are always worth visiting, so I rode up for some unexpected lunch. A simply superb leek and potato soup followed by strong local cheese. Considering the dinners I'd been feeding myself, this was luxury. It felt like I was carrying luggage on the way back. Roads so windy I near on ground to a halt on corners to save my footrests.

Back at the olive farm, the tent and gear had dried out and again the sunset appeared across the way. I'd stopped at the shop beforehand to pick up snacks and a Cornetto. I took my throne, red wine, book (*Cider with Rosie* by Laurie Lee) and peanuts out onto a verge to enjoy the falling sun as the last of its gaze hit the rows of olive trees beneath me.

Night fell and the wind picked up, whistling in the trees above. Not strong enough to reach my skin through two jackets, but enough to make me stop and listen. Then the rain came as two rather wet French ladies pulled up next door and started unloading their things. They declined my offer to help, so I retreated to the dry of my tent to take shelter. Later, as the rain cleared, I headed to the wooden shower block in my towel and met them again. Both thanked me for the earlier offer, then one blocked my way to the shower and proceeded to sing me a song in the only English she knew. I'd have been able to concentrate on the lyrics and recite them here for you if she wasn't but an inch from my face. I shifted my weight from side to side in an awkward stance, aware that all I had on was a small travel towel. The smell of her breath and the feel of splattered saliva were off-putting to say the least. She repeatedly said, "Listen!"

to ensure my full attention. *I am!* I stood in the light drizzle for a long while, grasping my towel for dear life.

The following morning they cornered me again, this time fully clothed. They were dry and singing in French, reciting Frédéric Mistral. (I didn't know who he was at the time – the 1904 Nobel Prize winner in Literature, don't you know.) After her rendition she took an interest in Jimmy and gave him a hug and fondle. She was seventy years young, mind, which to be camping in a tent and travelling France in a small car was a great accolade to her. She was entertaining, and Jimmy thoroughly enjoyed it.

7
SOGGY BATTER

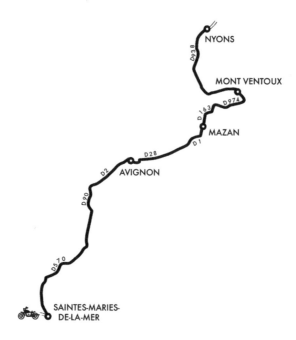

Mont Ventoux. A long gradual incline as the road looped around the mountain before reaching 1,909 metres at its peak. (Ben Nevis, the tallest peak in the UK, is 1,345 metres.) I frequently passed climbing cyclists as the piercing cold magnified. At the peak, after parking up I kept my helmet on and visor down for the most part, due to the sheer force of the wind. Looking out north-eastwards, I saw the white-topped Alps in the distance with ageing tree colour variations of circumjacent land at the base of the bright sky canvas, tainted only by aeroplane vapour trails that scratched the heavens. A highly recommended ride. For the road and the view follow the D974 all the way round. Either direction is great. Be prepared to encounter many cyclists attempting the Tour de France climb.

After the descent I took the country roads towards Avignon, the capital of the Vaucluse region and the Côtes du Rhône. Leaving the bike parked and luggage guarded by Jimmy, carrying my third-hand, five-quid Hein Gericke tank bag I wandered around this intriguing city in search of history and culture. Result. I found an Irish bar to watch Ireland v Russia (35–0 FT) and had half a Guinness, which hadn't been poured in a while. Can you believe I had to request they put the game on? Post priority rugby, I went for a curious wander about the city. An array of Gothic buildings and narrow streets could have kept me occupied for hours, but carrying my tank bag and worrying about Jimmy's safety meant I made my way back to the bike. Another place added to the list to complete the tourist circle. Jimmy was grand, although eager to move on.

To the coast!

A seaside town. A Weston-super-Mare with a French twist. Like dipping your battered cod in onion soup; it seems like a good idea at the time, but it quickly becomes soggy and grotesque. This was Saintes-Maries-de-la-Mer.

It was a picturesque ride in, through a natural park across flat plains with high grass and roaming wild horses. Flamingos operated in the area but I saw none wild. The rides in and out were by far the best parts of the place.

I stopped for coffee at a beach bar late in the afternoon upon arrival. Not just unimpressed but disappointed by the surroundings of the town and the price of the coffee, I regretted riding down here, for a moment.

A gem of a campsite turned up ten minutes outside of town on the D85A. A manual barrier was down on the entrance as I arrived, with no signage or sign of life. I lifted the barrier and rode through, closing it behind before approaching a couple, their Swiss VW and two dogs across the field. At this point I didn't know we'd be conversing later over dinner and drinks. I was informed that the farmer turned up as and when to collect payments, and I can make myself at home.

Jimmy was happy and took residence in the tree above the tent, following the fall of the sun across the high grass fields in that arresting, South of France way that it does. I'd noticed this over the previous days, having not been before, in between the overloaded scenery. After dinner and a glass of wine, I dragged my chair over to the camp of Rob and Andrea, the Swiss–Dutch couple I'd encountered earlier. Andrea spoke great, unpractised English as Rob made many a joke without needing the full vocabulary. Plus, Andrea did a great job at translating, almost more fluid the more the wine rippled. My name was now "Mr Jim" as we laughed long into the night, talking of differences at home and re-enacting stories from our pasts. Andrea was a professional driver. She recalled a story – on the prompting of Mr Rob, may I add – about one of her daredevil clients attempting to ride up a down escalator in their wheelchair, knowing full well what they were up to. As I pictured the scene, I looked up to the dark sky and continued until I could see the hedge behind me as I toppled over backwards, legs shaking in the air. Time to call it a night.

After breakfast of coffee, chorizo, cheese and bread, and continuous laughter about the night before, I threw the rope ball for the dogs. The first throw landed high in a tree. I went red and felt bad, but Andrea and Rob just laughed, prompting us to spend half an hour trying to retrieve it, with little else to do for the day. First, I threw juggling balls, but they weren't heavy enough. One of the campers, a rock-climbing Danish women, gave it a whirl and hung upside down in the tree for a while. We then tried throwing Rob's sheathed, custom-made axe, which got stuck up the tree as well. Back to the juggling balls, with no success.

Rob spotted that the recently arrived campers had a van with poles for their awning. Some negotiation later, down it came, and tied together they were long enough to prod out the axe and toys. A successful morning's activity to earn us the staple-diet lunch.

A little hungover with a heavy head after Operation Dog's Ball Retrieval, I ventured into town to check out the market and picked up a dark-red clay coffee cup. I'd had enough of drinking out of plastic and I had space to carry it. Outside the sandstone church in the centre of the town a party was taking place. I sat and watched the enjoyment on everyone's faces as people linked arms, moved and sang in the church's shadow. It was a while before I realised that the majority of people dancing had varying disabilities. A man without a hand and only two fingers on his other reached into his pocket to get something out at the request of his friend. He dug deep for some time. Then, facing his friend, his hand emerged, his two fingers swearing in a V. There was loud laughter from all, including his friend, and I couldn't help but join in as it was a joke I was familiar with. On the way back to my bike, groups of men played boules in the central sandy square, and fat red tourists (somewhat resembling myself) sat outside the bars, drinking beer.

At the camp that night, I was invited to join the office-working, rock-climbing Danish girls as one walked precariously on their slackline between two trees, but thought better of it. I joined the Swiss again for a quieter beverage.

I popped back to my tent to put on trousers after enduring shorts long after dark.

"You English are cold, huh? We Swiss, strong," Rob said in his deep voice, followed by inbreath chuckles.

"But this morning, you were cold," I questioned back in response with flippant pointing.

"Ah cold, yes," he agreed, rubbing his arms.

Then he whispered in close: "But do not tell my wife."

Prost to you both, Andrea and Rob, and dogs Boco and Charlie.

notes

- there is a local bird sanctuary on the main road which was good for a couple of hours to see some exquisite birds
- southern coast of France wasn't for me. Too touristy. So I planned a route inland
- "prost" is "cheers" in German

8
TALLER THAN THE
EIFFEL

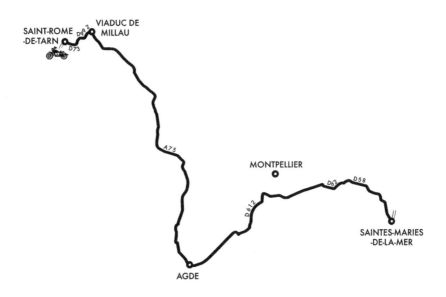

Recalling conversations from the ferry queue on the way over, I remembered one of the motorbike riders mentioning the Viaduc de Millau was a worthwhile visit. We'd not got very far before stopping in an open café-bar to watch England v Argentina (39–10 FT).

As I sat at the bar watching the TV above the coffee machine, many characters came and went. They were all middle-to-older-aged men who had popped in for a swift coffee, going about their day. One chap lingered for a few mid-morning glasses of red wine and soon had a red face similar to mine. Looking away from the game for just a moment, I spied him winking at the two bartenders. Whilst my French was poor, the inappropriate flirting was obvious.

A direct route to the bridge would have taken less than two hours, but I wanted to ride through Sète and Agde on the coast and enjoy a slap-up seafood lunch. I was thinking lobster, crab, prawn salad; the works. The road joining the two looked intriguing from the map as water surrounded each side of the long, straight road, but it wasn't the desired detour I was after. The train track ran parallel with high hedges so I couldn't see anything. Without finding a single restaurant worth its salt in Agde, my seafood lunch was a tin of tuna and an apple on crackers in a desolate car park by the beach.

Inland from Agde after getting fuel, the A75 motorway quickly arrived (toll-free until the bridge), which took us all the way to the Viaduc de Millau. It was fast, straight, windy and cold. A front screen on the bike would have been a godsend. Almost as soon as I hit the motorway, I pulled off for a rest and snacks.

Sat down, surrounded by large rocks on the edge of a knee-high grassy field by a service station and overlooked by a wooden cross on a rocky mound, I brewed coffee and closed my eyes. My earlier shop-bought baguette, cheese and chorizo accompanied the brew. I opened my eyes to the motorbike roar of a Harley Davidson parade riding past, entering the slip road.

I gave up nodding to each of the thirty riders after the first few as it felt like I was at a rock concert.

The Viaduc de Millau is an engineering specimen. Taller than the Eiffel Tower, it takes top spot as tallest bridge in the world.

Even if bridges don't interest you, it's a thought-provoking sight as it joins the raised sides of the wide valley. To cross the bridge there's a toll. Mastercard failed to work on this automated machine as well, which confirmed my distaste for tolls. I didn't understand the response in French after pushing the big red button, so I waited patiently for a minute before walking the bike back into the next lane to try a new machine. Still nothing. A man came out to assist manually with a card machine, holding up the traffic behind before waving me through. It was possible to ride beneath the bridge without having to pay, as I found out afterwards, but it was worth paying to ride across. The information centre was undoubtedly worth visiting as it portrayed the project well enough to gasp at the construction method. I bumped into the Harley parade again in the car park. All well over fifty, in their Harley-branded bandanas and boots, they gave Jimmy a wave as his droopy mouth caught the wind when I left. If he could dribble, it would've gone everywhere. Old boys and their toys. It didn't occur to me at the time that I looked the spit image at twenty-five.

I reached the valley below and felt dark falling. My energy drained as the light left and my headlight was switched on. The viaduct dominated the sky above as I rode underneath, heading out of town. There were many motorbike repair shops in Millau, which were fortunately not needed yet. I headed south-west on the winding D roads with no margin for error, in the direction of a campsite in the village of Saint-Rome-de-Tarn.

A fresh gravel track neighboured the River Tarn at the bottom of the village. The campsite shopfront was closed, but the camping enclosure entrance was open on the opposite side of the track. A group of lads sat around the corner of the building on a concrete patio in front of sliding double doors. Without stopping, I rode into the site. Drips of drizzle ran off the thick old branches on the trees. They would provide sufficient cover in summer months, but on a wet day in October, they held the moisture like a hot shower in a windowless room. What looked like permanent static homes and caravans were scattered around, but there were no tents or other signs of life. A car pulled in and tailed me through the campground. I didn't stop for it but carried on, glancing in my mirror as I turned the corners. There was no attempt at flashing their lights or honking the horn, just the lingering tail. I was pretty shot at this time of the day and didn't need this. I arrived back at the entrance and exited the site, turning right to follow the riverbank and losing my tail as they turned left. By the riverside, heading towards a clubhouse of sorts, a motorhome was parked up and a few tents looked like they'd been there a while. All with fishing rods cast out and proper comfortable camp set-ups. They were not particularly pleased with a loud motorbike casually cruising by, frightening the fish, but it didn't cross my mind at the time as I smiled through my helmet. Camping was allowed by the bank but for competition fishers only, not a loud motorbike and a monkey. I spun the Shadow round and rode back to enquire about the campsite and that lingering car.

"Leffe?" one of the lads offered, after we cleared up that it was okay for me to set up camp. I was relieved to hear it was them tailing me.

"Oui, merci beaucoup." I accepted.

Another long day on the bike deserved a strong, cold Belgian beer.

It was a Saturday night birthday party in a rented village hall just outside the campsite. I was invited to stay for the celebration. The earlier fatigue lifted and I was up for the social. Having missed the main shop in Millau, I purchased a couple of takeaways from a café in the village after making camp. Once these were drunk, at no point was my hand empty. I was offered a fresh beer all night long as soon as I tilted my head back to ninety degrees. Few spoke English, but almost everyone tried as they got me proper pished. I brought up my contention against prepaid fuel and was light-heartedly informed by one chap that "French people would just drive off without paying".

More partygoers arrived throughout the night. Everyone was originally local to this village but had since left for work or study. Vast numbers had travelled back across France for the event, a real family occasion. The rented room was packed and spilled out onto the patio. French techno music bellowed out across the river and the lights led the way. The parents and their friends, however, seemed sceptical of my presence having just turned up. With no fluent French to charm them, I did my best to avoid them. The younger crowd around my age vouched for me and assured them I was "nice", as I heard them say. At one point they wanted to know my taste in music so I reeled off The Cat Empire's "Brighter Than Gold", the first thing I could think of. As soon as I mentioned it, I wasn't quite sure what reaction it would get after the techno sessions I'd endured. The answer became clear thirty seconds later when it was switched back. Several beers deep, one toke of a locally rolled cigarette turned out to be a showstopper. I stumbled back to my tent at about 3.30 a.m. with the party still in full flow. Falling asleep still wearing my motorbike jeans, boots out the door.

The second Sunday in France and I needed the rest. By late morning I shadily left my tent on foot (not in a fit state to ride as I was completely hanging baskets) and walked up the hill, with several breaks, to the small village shop to pick up lunch, dinner and snacks, along with a warm crusty white baguette from the bakery (a French baguette back home; just a baguette in France). More cheese for lunch with chipolatas, tinned veg and rice for dinner. I spent the day wrapped in a blanket by the riverbank, listening to music and finishing my book, later retreating to the tent porch to cook dinner in shelter from the rain. The rain flew sideways into the porch so I wheeled the Shadow in front of the tent and fashioned a porch extension using a spare tent groundsheet and bungee hooks. The dark evenings started early.

notes

- an extra ground sheet or tarpaulin is highly recommended for a bit of breathing room in wet weather

9
BREAKING, ENTERING, AND LEAVING NO TRACE

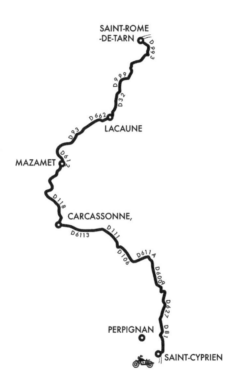

With no rugby to stop for, and finally a clear head, I hit the road early doors; like starting work on a Monday morning, but instead of the usual dread of returning to work, I was beaming ear to ear with my new commute. I drew a straight line on the map south to Carcassonne, weaving across it back and forth through two nippy natural parks, similar small towns and gallant green pastures. This was an extremely tough day. The cold was fierce and fired explosive blows as I roamed the region. My recollection of the morning's ride is as foggy as the mist of those moments, but there are certain parts I won't forget. The constant want for warmth, the serious consideration of pretending I was wearing a wetsuit so that I could relieve myself as I rode, and arriving at Lacaune on the wrong side of the road. I pulled out of a junction, turned right, and on autopilot I steered us over to the left-hand side. I had travelled a hundred metres into the centre of town before an oncoming car straight ahead was in my lane. *What are you doing there, mate? Shit!* My mind snapped at me in sync with their pressed horn, drowning the deep chugging of the bike. Upon reflection, I'd spent the morning on single-track roads with no other vehicles. The fog was thick and the weather so raw that I'd succumbed to losing concentration. Time for a rest for rider safety, I heard my IAM advanced course rightly whisper in the wind.

Entering the final stretch from Mazamet to Carcassonne, I hoped each descending road would be the last, leaving the cold of the elevation for the warmth of sea level. Yet around the bend another rising gradient induced a desire to ride faster. Jimmy's ginger locks were clamped with ice.

The wide valley of upper Aude was a sigh of relief. The warmth arrived like stepping off a plane in a hot country. A fast, curvaceous road, the D118 was welcomed before backing off the accelerator for the built-up area of Carcassonne. I took a rest stop outside the vast inner walls of the fortified city, then, as the sun emerged and coffee brewed, I fully thawed out to take a short stroll around the city's mazed medieval streets rich in history. Similarly to Avignon, I'd love to go back as a fully fledged tourist.

Almost two hours to Perpignan via Port Leucate. Home time for schools, as buses pulled out onto main roads frequently without looking. Not the most relaxing of drives, but at least I was warm(er).

An uneasy evening topped off a difficult day as I could not find an open campsite for the life of me, and was quite ready to ride on to Spain at this point. Wild camping was an option, but I needed a full shower and change as I'm sure a little pee came out earlier when I considered releasing the floodgates. There were many van parks still in operation but they didn't allow tents. Concrete and tents aren't a great combination. I'd gone too far into Perpignan and the built-up coast of Saint-Cyprien to consider a wild camp inland again, as darkness was falling fast and I still needed to eat. This became priority number one, so I picked up dinner: a fresh baguette, tomato and brie for a sarnie, plus a cheeky small bottle of red to see me through wherever my head would rest that night.

By this time it had gone 9 p.m. I approached a tourist campsite fitted with a water park towering above the high fences. A code-controlled security gate stood tall, with a second red-and-white barrier visible on the other side. The gates were shut. Reception was closed. I saw no way through.

I loitered outside for only a minute, my mind relaying ideas back and forth, rating them in terms of suitability and recklessness, before a car approached and the driver typed in the code. *I can't see what they put.* I'd not considered this unexpected arrival. With only a second to decide, I took the opportunity, tailed their bumper, and followed them through into the unknown.

With the best of intentions (but in all honesty with minimal effort), I tried to find a member of staff to announce my arrival, but to no avail. I tiptoed through the all-season stationary caravans to find a pitch, settling on a small, grassy and uninhabited corner section smack bang in the middle of the park. To be safe, Jimmy would sleep in the tent tonight instead of the typical tree perch. If I'd arrived in the light of day, I was sure I would have been directed elsewhere as mine was the only tent, surrounded by a hundred mobile homes. I enjoyed some more of my filled baguette, cowering in my tent to avoid passers-by, before having a swift shower and an early night, with the alarm set for before dawn.

I'd unpacked the bare minimum the night before to allow for an early escape. I was up and packed down in half an hour, setting a record. I wheeled the bike through the site. There was no movement to be seen outside the homes. With the gates in sight but not yet open, I prepared by sending a quick Snapchat to mates, unsure of how this was going to pan out; at least people would know my last known location. I put my helmet on, checked everything was secure; poised, ready to pounce. Movement ahead. I was a hundred feet away, give or take, and pulled in next to a hedge, out of view from reception. I intently examined a staff member walking up the steps. I was startled by my peripheral vision. A young girl walked past and stared, and I awkwardly glanced back, hoping, no praying, that she wouldn't give me away. Danger averted as she strolled off into the depths of the campground.

The main gate opened but the barrier remained fastened. I noticed it was just possible to get round the barrier on two wheels. I waited some seconds to ensure the main gate stayed open, otherwise I'd be wedged between the two. Out came the choke; I checked neutral and turned the key. With a deep breath, thumb poised over the starter button like a fighter pilot, I committed. The engine roared into action. A short pause as the V-Twin turned over and steadied, and I was off. The barrier beckoned as I was a margin over the camp speed limit of 10 km/h. I could sense Jimmy urging me to go faster. I took no glance towards the reception on the right. I slalomed around the closed barrier, through the gate and into freedom.

"Yee-haw!" I bellowed, as if I was riding my stallion like a hustler fleeing a bank robbery in a Western. Only riding the Shadow escaping a campsite. How times have changed.

The sea air had never been so potent, and the grin on my face turned to a loud cheer as I released the power of the engine. I checked the mirrors before turning the corner to ensure no one was in pursuit. All clear.

As I sat on the dock of the bay to start the day, the sun rose over parched sailing boats stuck in low tide. The coffee whistled, breaking my gaze as the bin men did their rounds. A small portion of leftover bread and cheese made brekkie.

notes

- for clarification, I would never have done this at a small or family-run campsite. I was not prepared to pay €25 a night for this tourist trap where I didn't even get to use the waterslide

10
AU REVOIR, FRANCE

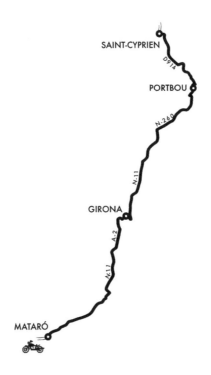

Spain! The D914 coastal road was well worth the run. Not one for speed but a slow ride with many corners, with cars frequently approaching in the middle of the road. (I could well be talking about any corner in Spain, or Europe, or anywhere in fact.) Each bend was the next photo opportunity. I stopped for photos at the old France–Spain border, which was lathered with graffiti and posters, layer upon layer. Up until 1985, passports were required. At the time of travel there was no need for border control at this Schengen-area land crossing. At the time of writing, post Brexit and with Covid regulations, this may have changed for UK passport holders.

The GoPro went on, capturing the blue sign proclaiming España before I descended a spiralling hill through an arch of cameras and past the first fuel stop this side of the border. The plunge down towards Portbou by the glistening Mediterranean Sea of the Costa Brava region was dazzling, aided by the sun's rays bouncing off the succulent sands of the rural beaches I passed. I stopped at one to brew another coffee and soak up some sun without a helmet or leather jacket on, revealing my pasty white skin to the Spanish sun at last. Jimmy's ginger locks glimmered. I was looking forward to practising my Spanish (although I stopped in Figueres just inland for lunch and I managed to order in French). I'd have liked to have leisurely followed the coastal roads all the way down through Spain, but my only real appointment of the trip was fast approaching: to pick up Tasha from Málaga airport on Friday 18 October for a different adventure entirely.

On to Barcelona. I'd weighed up a few options about getting and staying there, and what to do with the bike and luggage:

1. Hostel or hotel with secure parking

2. Hostel with external secure parking nearby
3. City campsite
4. Camping north of Barcelona and riding in daily

All of which involved riding into the city, which I wasn't particularly keen on doing. I'd heard of the madness of mopeds there.

5. Camping Barcelona. A secure campsite in Mataró designed for visiting the city, with a free shuttle there and back a few times daily. About forty minutes north of Barcelona. It was cheaper and easier to leave the bike and belongings there, bus it into the city with just a day bag, get a hostel for the night, then bus it back the next day. No riding in the city, either. Result!

The campsite ground was gravel, with strict, numbered slots in rows for camping. The odd tree stood alone in a more liberal arrangement. I took my spot next to one, counting a handful of camper vans not far across the site, and soaked in the afternoon sun.

I was invited for a drink that night by a group of German frat boys as they partied in their van in the slot opposite before heading back to college later that week. Après-ski classics blared out all night and smoke seeped out through the window cracks. What one would call in the industry a "hotbox". I declined their invite with a giggle but remained polite and soon drifted off in preparation for an early morning.

11
BƏRSƏLÓNƏ

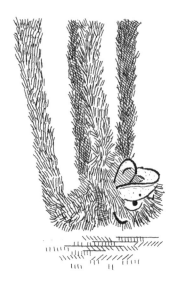

Barcelona. What a city.

Jimmy was left to guard the bike back at camp. For some reason, I didn't feel confident carrying him around all day without the meaty motorbike. I boarded the bus, my dry bag packed with spare underwear, a pair of socks, a shirt, toothbrush and paste, notebook, moisturiser, pocket Spanish phrase book and phone charger, with hat and sunglasses on my head. I left the shuttle bus to have a coffee and pastry in Plaça de Catalunya, a famous square. Sat outside the grand corner café, vibrations rallied up through my legs, into my stomach and out through my arms. My first thought was about my insides, post-black coffee and cigarette, but as I saw someone disappear in a black box like something out of Harry Potter, I realised it must be the metro station below. Regardless, I shuffled off to the café's downstairs bathroom just to be sure.

According to the advice given by a chap on the shuttle bus from camp, the tour bus was the best route around the city. It was around €30 for one day and €40 for two days. Hop on, hop off, hop on, hop off, as many times as you like. It offered an up-close-and-personal top-deck tour, so I rode the bus for a full lap to get an idea of the scale and to note which places I wanted to visit, with a booking already made for Sagrada Familia the following day.

notes

- tour bus around the city is highly recommended as the two routes access everywhere you'd want to go

Down by the port, the likeness of the World Trade Centre to a ship was relayed via the tour guide on our individual headphones. Two American ladies sat in front gasped in agreement:

"Oh my gosh, it does look like a boat, yes!"

They were right. The WTC does look rather like a boat. However, they pointed at a large ferry docked in the harbour and I didn't have the heart to tell them otherwise.

During the tour I added the Gothic cathedral, Barceloneta, Camp Nou, Tibidabo, Park Güell, Botanical Gardens, Santa María del Mar church, La Pedrera (Casa Milá) and Casa Batlló (Mi casa es su casa = My house is your house) to my list of places to see. Yet before I could enjoy any of these famous sights, I added to my list of top-deck bus blunders as we passed the Olympic port. The American ladies were long gone and there had been a few rotations in the seats since. The bus was full at each stop. A French lad about the same age sat next to me, with – I presumed – his mother, who sat in front of him. I knew he was French because the audio slot was on my side so I offered to plug his earphone cable in the socket of his choosing.

"Which channel?" I asked.

"Eleven," he said, which was the slot labelled with a French flag. He then conversed in French with his mother as the tour bus rolled past the redeveloped Bogatell Beach, which was empty on that overcast day save a few walkers. At that moment I turned my gaze in his direction and caught a front-row-seat show, as a plethora of dandruff specks leapt from his mother's mop of hair, flew in slow motion, then crash-landed into her son's face. Sparks flew everywhere. He had wisely kept his mouth closed and saved face as he pretended not to notice until I looked away. Obviously I quickly looked back to catch him wiping the debris away from his top lip. Inside I was in pieces but I didn't let it show apart from a small tear. I made a discreet note in my book.

I missed the stop for Tibidabo (a beautifully placed theme park high on a hill with stunning views of the city and coastline, supposedly) as the bus stop looked like a junction. With no time in my two days to get back there, I begrudgingly crossed it off my list and sat back down. It was a long route to the next stop: Antoni Gaudí's La Pedrera building, an earlier visit than planned, followed by his Casa Batlló a few streets down. Impressive works of art from the outside, but being too cheap for an admission ticket, I have no comments on the inside tours. *Spectacular, I'm sure.*

After travelling back on the bus to the start of the loop at Plaça de Catalunya, I got off and walked down La Rambla and into the side streets. Men sold massage services and drugs as tourists littered the streets along a catwalk of market stalls with prize-winning head-sized peppers hanging in large bunches. They didn't deter from the vibrant atmosphere but I couldn't help but feel trapped there as a tourist. I stopped in an over-my-price-range bar for tapas plates and caught some of the Wales v Fiji fixture (29–17 FT) on my phone. I left before the game ended thanks to a large open-collared Aussie businessman with a whooping cough who sat next but one to me at the bar. I thought the cause could have been the shellfish but a big inhale of phlegm through his nose proved otherwise. Lunch was finished.

In the direction of my hostel, numerous bars with outside seating taunted me until finally I stopped at one: Bar Mendizábal. The barman kindly gave me productive feedback on my Spanish as I sat in the small square in El Raval and watched the world go by. A large "Raval" tag was sprayed under the bar counter on the street-facing side in a decent design, unlike many of the tags on the adjoining building, which would have needed a ladder to reach. Each yearned for more space as they layered each other, messy and illegible to my eye.

I turned the corner with a bounce to my beery step, a few doors down from my hostel, my phone told me. I looked up and stopped in my tracks. Three police cars loitered outside. Lights flashed blue as they blocked the road. There was no movement. I scanned the area. It was still light as evening had not yet arrived, but the streets were empty. I didn't know Barcelona had empty streets. This was concerning. I know the hostel was cheap, but not that cheap. By accident had I snuck past a roadblock? Was something going down? I approached for a closer look but nothing gave the game away. My hostel neighboured the innocent-until-proven-guilty establishment hosting the Guàrdia Urbana. I took a deep breath and went in.

I greeted the hostel receptionist who'd just come off the phone. "Yo tengo una reservación para esta noche." (I have a reservation for tonight.) "Mi nombre es Jim Merryfield."

This was as far as the conversation went in Spanish because I didn't understand their reply.

"I had to cancel your reservation, Jim, because your credit card was blocked," they said in pristine English after we had cleared up that I couldn't speak Spanish.

"Can I have your passport, please, so I can create a new booking?"

"I don't have my passport with me," I said in embarrassment. I'd left it locked with my bike at camp.

"Right, okay. Well, I need it to make a booking. I'm sorry but I can't book you in without it. It's the law."

Shit. I wondered what on earth I was going to do. I replied with a blank expression, looking deep into their auburn eyes to tempt out empathy. This would apply to every hostel in the city. I remembered, being the organised traveller that I am, I had a photo on my phone. I pleaded with them to accept it. After a deep sigh and an interminable wait, finally they did. I paid with a different card, decided I'd deal with the credit later, took some advice on nightlife and left the unrequired items in the room before heading towards the port in the direction of Barceloneta. The police were gone. At the end of the hostel's street was a building called Baghdad. Supposedly a nightclub but definitely a strip joint from the large bold images of nakedness outside. For the sake of my relationship, I can confirm I did not go in.

A cloudy, warm afternoon persuaded an enjoyable walk past the Mirador de Colom by the waterfront. Private boats boasting wealth moored in the harbour, and further along, an exclusive club exhibition for the wealthy took place, where fancy cars and motorboats were lined up, protected by security. At the entrance was a large police presence, all chatting in a group, guns at hips, obviously busy. An Asian man fed a pigeon before getting swarmed by thirty of them, resulting in him throwing all the bread on the floor and running off. The cycle path was swarming with electric scooters and bicycles. A smiling elderly couple sharing a bike passed the large lobster statue, arms wrapped around each other, making hay while the sun shone. I couldn't help but reciprocate the grin.

Sat in a bar off a square in Barceloneta, I crossed it off my list then planned my evening. There was a gig in the Jamboree Jazz Club at 10 p.m., which wasn't far from my hostel. First port of call, to steady the sailing ship, I sank a supper of tapas in the midst of some small streets near the harbour, at El Callejón, a small home-cooking restaurant. Dark lighting covered cosy tables. I was particularly moist on arrival, as a non-forecasted downpour had instigated the choice of the cheaper poncho purchase over an umbrella which was an ill-advised, rushed decision. The place was early-evening empty when I arrived, except for a couple in the corner.

Fair play to the waiter. They were very patient with my attempt to order in Spanish. Smoked salmon with orange pulp was a winner. The meal hadn't particularly worked in sobering me up as I had two large glasses of delightful red wine to accompany it.

An after-dinner stroll and a couple of swift beverage stops later, I made my way to Jamboree.

The jazz show was due to start at 10 p.m. and I was worried I'd miss it. My pace quickened as I navigated the weaving streets. Multiple wrong turns later, I arrived with a minute to spare, hastily paid the man at the booth (€5, I think, or maybe €15) and made my way downstairs. Following a quick beer detour, I entered the main room. Exposed stonework formed the walls of the narrow cellar venue. Chairs were laid out in rows with the stage at the end. The word "Jamboree" was lit up behind the instruments. A grand piano, saxophone, drum kit and double bass lay lonely.

Six people were scattered around the sixty-plus seated room. It had crossed the start timeline and the band would be on any minute. *Surely they must be gutted at the poor turnout.* I questioned my own decision of being there, sat with the band's family members in the crowd. *I've come this far ...*

10.10 p.m. Thirty people had sat down. There was still no music.

10.25 p.m. The place was three-quarters full. Still no music.

10.30 p.m. Music. I'd not considered Spanish time.

Four young members of the band Tronik-Toni Saigi put on a great show. The pianist leading the show spoke in Catalan so I couldn't understand the song descriptions, but his delivery was done with passion regardless of the language barrier. Mesmerising jazz followed. A nervous, talented double bassist made mistakes in his solos but got an applause as loud as the others nonetheless, which was gratifying.

What time it was when I left, I don't know, but a few beers passed at least. The streets were the narrowest of the day, resulting in close contact with corner men stood selling whispers of items as I walked past. All were carrying a few cans of lager in a bag – *just selling cans of lager?*

As I turned a corner, I recognised the language as a man strolled with purpose towards me, shouting "You lying, cheating c***!"

A distressed woman and young lad were in pursuit ten feet behind. She retorted: "Your dad has just left me in a bar for two hours with a German bloke!"

And that was that. What a cracking holiday that sounded like.

I turned onto another backstreet. I don't know how long I'd been walking for but it appeared as though I'd walked in circles back to the Jamboree club, where I met the same whispering bloke on the corner, shaking his cans in my face. *No one wants a fizzy beer mate.* I felt again for the young lad enduring his parents' holiday.

I made it back to the hostel unscathed in the early morning, after taking a short stop on a local park bench to soak up the day and have a quick cigarette. Some shady characters at the park's perimeter gave me cause for concern, so I promptly made tracks back to the hostel.

Too early the next morning I was woken by an agitating alarm – not mine – that didn't turn off. The sound was muffled under a roommate's pillow but loud enough to wake my drowsy self. Before long he turned it off and I got back to sleep before being up again, ready for the 10 a.m. check-out.

Camp Nou and Sagrada Familia were booked for the day. Camp Nou housed an impressive collection of trophies, and through well-scripted photos and old football kit it portrayed the history of Barcelona Football Club. I would swap the tour for match-day tickets any day, although I got a selfie with a life-size cut-out of Lionel Messi as I wore my Winscombe rugby shirt, which I posted on social media with the quote: "Two great clubs. Two legends". Honestly, I hurried through, unlike the schools of fanatics. Although glad I went.

Next followed the Sagrada Familia, which is where I wanted to spend most of my time. The security was on high alert on entrance. I had to declare my Swiss penknife, a gift at fourteen, pleased to have it returned at the end. Inside and out, it was an incredible marvel. A hundred per cent recommendation from me; Antoni Gaudí did a fine job. Currently it's still being built, but this should not halt your visit as seeing the development was equally spellbinding. I'd especially recommend you take the time to read the museum and information section, which dives deeper into his methods linked to nature that were visible everywhere: "With intersecting hyperboloids, Gaudí transformed the neo-Gothic windows of the naves into a more natural structure. The results allow more light in and better distribute it." I read this off the informative plaque as it referred to a particular window that had similar features to a "microphotograph of the skeleton of a single-cell organism." Like the human bones, tibia and fibula on the outside of Batlló house, Sagrada Familia portrayed the slender, sprawled columns like trees with their branches, which was customary of Gothic cathedral columns. Yet Gaudí's columns, like trees, independently supported their own weight of ceiling, not relying on beams. If one fell, the others would not. The towers outside stood like the flower the Pride of Madeira, the spiral staircases shaped like the shells of snails. The stained-glass windows encompassed the sense of seasons and solstice, their warm and cold colours entwined.

I sat in the main hall for two hours in pure contemplation, making the occasional note as I allowed time for thought. There was usually plenty of time for this on the road, but this was different. The sensory input was so potent, it raised my scale of thought almost through this oppressively opulent sky-high ceiling and beyond. However, everyone became distracted by the bench security not letting some people into the central seating area. Unaware of the entry requirements, a Vicky Pollard-like character and her mate Rochelle in matching tracksuits kicked up a loud fuss, disturbing the shared tranquillity and magnificence.

One thought that kept recurring, other than that Gaudí must have been a genius, was *was it all necessary?* The structure was enormous. The cost even bigger still. As a religious building, would the money not be better utilised elsewhere for those people and communities that needed it most? I left with a feeling of insignificance, with no enlightening moment, but wondered what God's thought on it would be. If he/she/it/they/Gary had thoughts.

There was no German frat party when I turned in for the night back at Camping Barcelona. The bike was still padlocked to the tree and my passport was safe inside the panniers. As I lay my head down on the makeshift pillow, a fridge truck pulled up close by and charged all night at an alarming volume – something like a hundred-year-old generator due a service, it rattled, overheating and about to fall apart. Usually not fazed by this sort of thing, I waited an age in the hope of drifting off but bit the bullet and asked him to do something about it at roughly 11 p.m. and then again at midnight. The poor man was trying to sleep, like myself and other campers in earshot, but the sound was truly unmanageable. By 1 a.m. the staff had moved him elsewhere to a quieter spot, subsequently to annoy other campers.

Barcelona was truly brilliant, and a lot more time could have been spent there. The city became encapsulated to me by three men on one street in one minute, as I traipsed back to my hostel that first night in the early hours.

The first man was in a large roadside bin, removing anything that might be edible or valuable.

The second man with no shoes had long dreadlocks and strolled along the pavement, head held high as he played a four-stringed guitar and sang his heart out.

The third man, a shopkeeper, kicked leaves away from his shopfront with broom in hand.

The first man portrayed poverty and the activities people need to do to survive.

The second man represented the culture and love of music, regardless of stature.

The third man stood for proud wealth.

On that same street, at the same time, those people coexisted to create the unique, vibrant and diverse city that is Barcelona. I'll be back.

list of completion

- Gothic cathedral, ~~Barceloneta~~, ~~Camp Nou~~, Tibidabo, Park Güell, ~~La Pedrera~~, ~~Casa Batlló~~, ~~Plaça de Catalunya~~, Barcelona Botanical Gardens, Santa María del Mar church

12
WOLVES

Three weeks in I was leaving the outskirts of Barcelona for
Montserrat, a nearby Catalonian mountain range. I had to stop
for camping gas in a Decathlon sports shop as I'd be reverting
to one-pan camp meals after enjoying the mouth-watering food
Barcelona had to offer.

At Montserrat, the quiet, inclined hill after the town was not a fair representation of the tourist-swarmed car park at the top. I seriously struggled to park, almost unheard of for a bike. The bridge and top road were closed as weather severely impaired visibility for vehicles with the fallen veil, and as a result, foot traffic flowed up through the opaque-clouded mountain. There were superb lookouts on to the rolling green views below, so venturing off into the cloud didn't seem worth it at the time.

Free camping was on the cards that night after an enjoyably expensive Barcelona. I'd used park4night (a free camping location app; I'd used something similar when hitchhiking through Australia but had forgotten about it) which became super useful. I unearthed a spot that was back down the hill towards town, but then veered off halfway for a slow slalom ride on a narrow single track overgrown with bushes. After ten minutes I came out onto an opening that looked back at Montserrat and down to lower ground on the other side. The opening was stony under wheels. I stabilised with both legs while gently cruising the walkway. Before getting too deep in the bushes, I parked, then wandered around in search of a better area. It was not to be found and I was not up for riding elsewhere. A large white transit with roof racks was parked contrary to the mountainous rock face, securing the best spot on site. There was no owner visible but two terrifying, powerful wolves sat outside, growling under their breath. I dare not approach, and hoped they didn't either. They were mammoth dogs. I looked at Jimmy; I'd never seen him so muted. A GB number plate clung on to the transit's rear for dear life.

I cracked open a tinny (Aussie slang for a can of lager, usually preceded with "give us a fucking" and followed by "mate") and pulled out my throne to enjoy the last of the sun on my leather-less body. The Montserrat rock face stood struck with clouds pouring over the top like elephant toothpaste. The landscape was a mix of tough green bush and sandy ground that popped up in spots between the loose rock. It wasn't until I was erecting the tent that a tanned, curly haired man emerged from the GB-plated van in shorts and flip flops. With a beaming grin he came over to introduce himself and the dogs, Nancy and Sid, who in fact were elderly and ferocious-turned-friendly. In their prime they'd have been a force to be reckoned with. It turned out we had lots in common. We sat together and chatted most of the night over a few beers about the Magpies (Newcastle FC), the difficulties of learning Spanish, and which part of Spain would be best for him to buy a house. Having only just begun the Spanish leg of my trip I had no suggestions of places but took notes on some recommendations. He added smoking to the "difficulties of learning Spanish" list as he sparked up a spliff.

I woke in the morning to him walking the dogs, coffee cup and a joint in hand. "The breakfast of kings," he chuckled, beaming from ear to ear. Jimmy and I were off early to Siurana so declined his offer for breakfast. Don't drink and drive. Don't bud and bike.

There was one way in and out of Siurana, a small village perched high on a rock. The entrance road was surrounded by an explosion of trees. It felt like being in a giant bowl of cereal, crawling to reach the rim. It was a climber's dream, and they were out in force. A queue of cars waited to get into the car park, directed by stewards. I did as you're meant to do when on a motorbike, which is to ride to the front. I was waved right on through passing walkers coming and going from the car park. In the village itself there were multiple viewpoints in all directions around every corner of the cobbled streets. A couple of dried lakes lay below, yearning for rain. The buildings sat right on the cliff edge, save a few centimetres. When I learnt it was the last Muslim community to fall to the 1153 Christian invasion, it became apparent how that battle would have looked for the invaders. A constant crick in the neck for starters. How long it will be before the poignantly placed palaces perched on the cliff's edge crumble, along with the decaying rocks, I don't know, but they weren't far off needing intervention.

notes

- be sure to look out for the Moorish Queen's horse's hoofprint in Siurana. A beautiful place

I arrived late afternoon at La Fontcalda hot springs. The sun hid behind a peak in the distance as I embarked down the patchy track. Woodland stood tall on the left and a valley cliff sat down on the right, a small wooden fence separating me from the chasm. As I approached a mid-point, the scenery flipped 180 degrees around me, as if I was the centre of rotation. I followed the brow of the hillside before rolling down what looked like the edge. The route zigzagged back and forth multiple times with short, sharp hairpins on a loose-surfaced track. Potholes scattered the corners to make it even more challenging.

The springs themselves coiled between a break in the rocks, and what I thought was a cycle track on a bridge high above was another access point. A church, restaurant and BBQ area close to the car park were all closed and empty out of season. Unaware that I was hungry, the signs prompting food got me going. *I could eat.*

A family left as I walked down to the springs. Alone I was. I still opted for shorts in the pools but the wash was welcome. Fontcalda means "hot spring" in Catalan, but it didn't even reach lukewarm levels. I wondered whether the smell of sulphur came from my unused swim shorts but concluded it was the springs. Emerged up to my neck, eyes almost closing in deep relaxation, I spotted a snake enter the pool from the other side, maybe ten metres away. I thought I was all right with snakes, provided I knew where they were. I lost sight of it on entry, which ignited instant stress. I splashed about, making an almighty ruckus like a toddler in a paddling pool, then made a quick exit in the opposite direction.

Fully clothed, as I left the peaceful V-shaped river valley, another snake crossed my path a few feet in front. It reminded me of an encounter I had on a banana farm near Cairns, Australia, where I worked as a Banana Humper (official job title). A wedge would be cut into the tree with a machete, and the weight of the banana bunch – around 40–60 kg in Cairns – would slowly bring the tree down. In pairs, one cut and one carried, swapping tasks once the trailer had been filled. The quicker this happened, the longer the rest before the next trailer came, although often they were stacked up. My colleague cut the stalk of the bunch like he did every time, and I then proceeded to carry it off in a hurry. A snake fell from the tree and landed within reach of my next stride, which threw me off course and caused me to almost drop the entire bunch – unaware that non-poisonous snakes climb trees to flee from the poisonous bastards on the ground.

On the way up and out of the springs, just off the main road, there was a large recreational area with uneven grassy ground, and large wooden and concrete benches that had been left unloved and without care as they decayed. *A possible hidden spot to camp.* Far enough away from the main road but accessible for the bike. Two young Spaniards sat smoking a spliff, their helmets on a nearby moped. With good English and stern advice, they said not to camp there as it was a popular place for the police to visit. Not a wise idea for them to be smoking spliffs before riding, I thought. Mainly for their own safety on the road, let alone getting nicked. That wasn't my place to say!

Adhering to their advice, I rode off in the direction of a campsite. Dusk had arrived and the glow of the sun was visible behind mountains in the distance. The lay of the light and the few clouds made it look like the mountains were on fire, with smoke pouring out of the top like a live volcano.

The wind had picked up the dust, throwing it everywhere. Children scattered in the Campsite Tierra Altra play area without noticing the change in weather. A solo Swedish biker had seen me enter and scan the possible pitches as I rode around. After setting up, he came over to my tent for a chat and invited me out for grilled food in the nearby town of Bot. Still in my gear and with sweetcorn and rice already purchased for dinner, I respectfully declined, not thinking anything of the forward nature of his invite; as a lone traveller, company is usually welcomed. We shared good stories for half an hour before he left. After eating, I regretted not heading out for ribs and a chat, but I was ready to lie down and sleep.

Hiccup. Hiccup. Hiccup. *Oh, come on!* Without needing to stand on my head, my thumbs blocked my ears, and my forefingers, stretched in front like a pistol, closed my nostrils. This released the remaining three fingers on each hand to grasp my bottle of water and lift it to my mouth, tilting my head back. Whether it's the air pressure build-up or the concentration of trying to drink while looking like Zoidberg from Futurama, I don't know, but it works every time.

13
TOWER OF JOY

The first half of USA v Tonga (19–31 FT) kicked off before I shook the windswept, deep-red dirt from the tent. I packed up and, as usual, Jimmy hung out expressionless, mocking me. I didn't mind. I was the one who dragged him along. I slowly made the road at about midday and headed west. From Bot I rejoined the N-420 and continued onto the N-211, which were fast roads with plentiful room for overtaking. Layers of fluorescent, glowing trees in different shades of flourishing green were cast out either side. At a point signed at 1,200 m above sea level, the second stretch of the day's journey, the consistent olive greens turned to granular browns and the flat plains revealed emerging mounds on the horizon. I imagined it was like watching a tidal wave, far out to sea. Yet instead of being engulfed at the point of the wave, it calmly flowed beneath me and revealed once again the wavy, crinkled greenery of fields, and a wind farm further out, untouched by the gentle passing wave.

Castillo de Zafra. Arguably my favourite place of the entire trip. A long dirt track led the way, taken at crawling pace to save from spitting stones and slipping wheels. I weaved across it to follow the best route between the rocks, in a desperate state not to put my feet down. Obviously this was because I was pretending that the ground was lava; the only way I'd survive was to keep my feet off the ground. Tricky at a slow speed on two wheels. Alas, it was not possible, and my feet perished into a cloud of smoke as I swore to myself before laughing at myself for playing a child's game and loving it.

A car left as I arrived. Staring, inquisitive eyes passed me on the dreaded track, not expecting to see a monkey riding a motorbike. That left me alone, approaching the seemingly simple, imposing castle built on boulders. I raised my hand with my open palm facing me, then closed my ring and middle finger, held down by my thumb. Rock on. A perfect fit against the castle from afar, with minor squinting. In Spain, this hand gesture can refer to cuckoldry, which is fitting for the *Game of Thrones* storyline. Fans will be able to visualise it as Jon Snow's place of birth: the Tower of Joy. A fantastical setting, with high defence walls and tall towers at either end of the castle that sat crowned on the massive rock, adding to the difficulty of invasion. I could envisage the camera crew filming scenes and for a moment I felt compelled to re-enact the sword fight with sticks, but remembered how old I was. A twelfth-century relic restored. It was only possible to view the outside, as an inserted metal door was padlocked and reachable only by a metal staircase, but there was more than enough to admire as the castle rested afloat the surface of the surrounding hillscape.

Out of sight from the entrance track and castle, I set up camp before popping a bottle of wine purchased from Sant Josep Winery in Bot. No notation of the aged flavours at the time of tasting, but a lovely little number. Smooth sailing down the waterfall that was my gullet. I took a wander and perched on one of the many large rocks that towered the vicinity, with the castle in view. There was a working farm situated next door in the same field, with no fences to distinguish land ownership that I could see. The farm had utilised some of the large rock faces as part of their enclosure, half cave, half dry-stone wall, that lay uninhabited. Fresh sheep-shit fumes loitered, an invisible wave rising off the trodden dirt. A fading grey tree tilted over the rock edge with senility as its last strength rooted tight, interweaved between perfectly placed rocks.

With the sun setting I lay back and tried to soak up the day, content with the distance and route taken. Happy with the small wonders I'd encountered.

A deer emerged over the top of gathered boulders not so far away, poised in the shadow, motionless. Our eyes locked together in a stare. I glanced at the sunset and back. The deer disappeared into the night. The ever-faithful Jimmy stood firm on the motorbike as designated driver.

Splashing into the second – but, I'd like to note, slightly smaller – bottle of wine, the wind had become so strong that it felt as though it was going in one ear and out the other. The lower the volume left in the bottle, the higher the pitch became. I used my hand to block it and play a tune, bopping to the sound of the wind. After a failed attempt at beatboxing, and pretty pickled at this point, I wrote a poem of the scene I'd witnessed as it happened:

> As the sun drops, the shadows grow,
> castle admirers criss-cross up the steep hill,
> not knowing the rear car park is flatter.
>
> Beams enable the structure
> to stand tall and enlight the landscape.
> A cloudless sky except a hound chasing a hare.
>
> The towers absorb the last glow,
> the wind blows and the bushes chatter,
> a cyclist arrives late,
> tired engine,
> belly hungry,
> legs sore from the gravel paths.

One more push, then camp beneath the night-time pass.

Night had fallen by the time the cyclist turned up. The crickets were having a good ol' yarn as I watched the cyclist with head torch on set up their tent much closer to the castle and way further up the hill than I was. It was too far to greet whoever it was at that time of night, and their legs would have been too knackered to contemplate coming down to me. It would have been a stumble and mumble at best for the both of us. *We'll let this meeting slide.*

I stood up too quickly. I lost my footing and my hands went down. This disturbed my frail French mug from the safety of its crevice, which caused it to topple down the rock. Finding my feet, I heard it roll before I saw it. I trod in an articulate order, hitting solid, steady rock so I maintained my balance. I could've been one of those ferry foot passengers at that moment, but I reached the mug before it fell off the rock into the abyss. It was unmarked and intact. I breathed a sigh of relief.

With my belongings collected and bagged, I climbed down, each step reaching out into the darkness below. I tripped on the final hurdle and rolled onto the grass into safety. Nothing broken. Sat on the ground next to my tent, I finished off the last of the wine, scribbled some illegible notes about saving the mug from certain destruction, and thought about bed. I stood up and turned carelessly, stepping towards the tent. It only took one step. Crunch. The previously rescued mug lay beneath my size twelve boot, shattered into unsalvageable pieces. A deep sleep beckoned.

The morning bladder woke me early enough to see the moon shimmy behind a thick black cloud. An early indicator of what the day had in store. I got back in the sleeping bag to brew coffee and left the porch door open to admire the morning views as Jimmy, seemingly unfazed by the morning dew, soaked up his surroundings (literally absorbed the water in the porch). Amid the sheep shit I discreetly laid my own (properly buried) before packing up. I then noticed that the cyclist was long gone and I questioned if they'd turned up at all. *This Bot wine was strong stuff!*

On my way out of the remote region, back on the stony track, I met a tractor trailer head-on and I pulled in to let him pass. It was likely the owner of the farmyard I'd slept in. With haste I rode on, reaching tarmac and the safety of the open road.

Fields of wilted sunflowers summarised that self-inflicted feeling of the morning. Fortunately the roads were wide and empty, but rain clouds chased me as I checked my mirrors. Sunrays pierced through parts of the cloud as they stopped, paused for a moment to say hello, then disappeared, much like the deer the night before. Jimmy's head ferociously rattled up and down with the force of the wind. As I rode on, the sky fell darker and the sun wasn't just behind the clouds but out of range completely. Thus proving the earth is round. The heavens opened an hour after they forecast a forty per cent chance, just after I arrived in Molina de Aragón for coffee and breakfast at around 10 a.m. Sat outside at this point under suspect shelter, the other customers and I poured inside.

With a break in the rain, I set off, taking a left in town onto the CM-210, heading south through the Parque Natural de la Serranía de Cuenca towards Cuenca. I'd read about the roads in the park before the trip and had planned to spend a full day touring through, finishing late in a camping spot out of sight. As I entered the park, the skies opened and declined to stop for hours, so I took the quickest route available. My eczema had started to play up as the wet clothes rubbed. I had done pretty well with it thus far. But now my skin itched, ass to shoulder, dry and red from the chafing.

The roads swayed in and out of valleys, past colossal trees and recreational areas, with every degree of angled corner going. It was a play area for the bike, but being sodden to the bone from the get-go took the fun away. Birds of prey circled high above the trees dodging raindrops, not fazed by the weather.

As I came out of a valley onto a straight section, the scene of a car crash had recently unfolded. A neglected white caddy van with a company logo was upended, the front caved in, lying on the opposite side of the road and facing the wrong way – hopefully with no one inside. A small Fiat followed fifty metres further along, equally written off and on its side. Three men stood by, looking on. One had managed to give up the cigarettes, it seemed, as he spat out sunflower seeds. The other two were chugging their ciggies hard. Two more cars had pulled up in assistance so I decided a wet, teary Englishman would have been of little help.

The sun arrived when I landed in Cuenca, which oh my days was welcomed. I pulled in for a swift park bench visit to swap wet clothes for dry ones and to wring out my socks, before locating a food market online. After a while spent roaming the streets looking for a shop, I gave up and took the advice of a helpful citizen. A few minutes later I walked into Mesón El Tormo, a small meat speciality bar with a restaurant next door.

A fire grill for meat sat up on the back counter. Warmth. Food. Wine. Lovely.

A little beaten by the day, I couldn't help myself. I indulged in prawns, patatas bravas, bread and roasted vegetables without hesitation. I was gutted. I thought I'd ordered meat from the grill. It had been one of those days. I was well under the drink–ride limit, but I decided I was done for the day and pulled up park4night for some inspiring camping spots out of town.

With provisions from a local grocery shop I then spent the next hour riding up and down the N-420 trying to find a suitable spot. I found an off-road possibility and took it at speed to get up and over the mound, scraping the Shadow's bottom on the dirty deck. *I need water.* Supplies were low and wouldn't last me, unaware that I was about to find a freshwater spot right by a river. I jumped back on and found Calle Agua (Water Street) in the small village of Altarejos. A water fountain stood in the centre, ready to serve. With bottles filled, I left the village and settled for a gorgeous remote area down by Río Júcar.

In the midst of trees and canary yellow leaves I turned on the speaker, with zero consideration for any potential listener before unpacking. Out came the throne from the tightly packed bike. I then grasped the fully stocked food bag, and my apple, kiwi and orange toppled out. I was stepping in the process and timed it to perfection, booting the fruit off in acute angles. The apple shot off the furthest into the long grass. I collected the unbruised kiwi and orange with ease, then surveyed around for the apple. All three were in my hands just as "You Wish" by Nightmares on Wax came on the speaker, and up the volume cranked. If you don't know it, it's a roll-your-shoulders, knees-up and get-a-groove-on sort of tune. So that's what I did. I started bobbing my head, juggling the fruit and throwing terrible shapes as I joined the music, spit balling noises, succumbing to the natural reaction to start juggling with any three objects encountered.

A bitter wash sat down in the river soothed my thirsty skin. I focused on my breath, feeling the rush of water flow around me, before moisturising head to toe, wrapping up warm and sticking on a brew. I put rice on to boil, popped Jimmy in a tree, and admired the scenery as the music became gentler, in tune with the surrounding autumnal nature. Leggy trees and stout bushes. Fallen leaves and rising branches. A wide river and thin ripples. Closing my eyes, it's always visible. The famous Spanish winds played games in the trees, this time more consistent, like a motorboat chugging down the river.

14
DON'T SPARE
THE HORSES

The frost woke me up first thing. I lay cocooned in two sleeping bags (the second purchased from Decathlon), a flowery pink blanket donated from Patrice, beanie hat, socks, two jumpers, thermal leggings and jeans. *Loud music immediately* was my first thought to get the blood flowing. "Everybody Loves the

Sunshine" by Takuya Kuroda wasn't right for the moment, so I skipped on to "Morning Glory" by Poldoore which was much more fitting.

I shook the ice off the outside of the tent and looked at Jimmy sat on the bike. His fur was tangled with crisp icicles. I attempted to wash the pans in the flowing river with my fingers as a scourer, but it was too cold. My hands hurt. They had turned white and throbbed, so the pans went away dirty. I tucked my hands under my armpits and jumped around, splitting the low-lying mist, encouraging my blood to flow. The feeling in one hand returned as it warmed whilst squatting over a dug hole in the long grass for nature's business, which took me back to taking a shit in the bush when working the fence lines in the Australian outback. The warmth of the pindan soil rising accompanied by the sound of a thousand flies that resonated between both sets of cheeks. Then all I could think about was heading south as quickly as possible for warmer sands.

I had half a bottle of red left over from the day before. I'd been getting the smaller ones most of the time or the odd bottle of beer. *Maybe I'd reached my holiday limit?* It was a corked bottle instead of the usual cost-effective screw top. This made transportation all the more difficult. As drinking it for breakfast was not an option, I scratched my head. *Where on earth will I put this safely on the bike for the day?* Jimmy stared back at me with his usual blank expression. This time, he gave me an idea. As a puppet, he has an arsehole the size of an arm: the perfect stash place for a bottle to keep it upright. Up it went and I strapped it in. I'm sure I heard his squeaker go and saw his expression change. Sorry for that image, but it is what it is.

Without a shadow of a doubt this was the coldest day so far. Although I'd said that a few times. My now numb hands struggled to grip the bars and my toes wiggled ferociously of their own accord to keep the blood flowing, until they couldn't be wiggled any more. My face was scrunched up. I dared not move my head because a gust of frosty air would worm its way into the gap in my neck sleeve, slithering down to my ears, nibbling my neck, then into my layered torso. It sends a shiver down my spine recollecting it. I had to take the motorway. It was the only way to make up the distance and be rid of this harsh landscape.

Before boarding the E-5, I stopped for an espresso and elevenses pastry. It was a large restaurant-café, by no means full as ten locals stood around the bar area. I was greeted by the fugliest (fuck ugliest) little dog as I turned the corner to the front door. It truly shocked me with its dishevelled face and skew eyes, this unfortunate but innocent-enough-looking dog. Not sure if it could see me or just smell me, I shuffled past, back against the wall, just in case it was a ferocious guard dog. I survived.

On to the E-5. The perpetual chill was still extreme and after an hour or so I hit a mental wall. I felt as though my mind was leaving me as I loitered behind a truck at roughly the speed limit, not aware or even capable enough to pull out and overtake as my eyes opened and closed in a sequence that favoured the latter. I was going under. I could feel it. A dangerous place to have had this experience. I came round long enough to open my visor to receive the wet-fish slap of the wind. I sang the first song I knew a few words of to keep myself focused. "In Dublin's fair city" – I started to shout – "where the girls are so pretty, I first laid my eyes on sweet Molly Malone. As she wheeled her wheelbarrow, through the streets broad and narrow ..." And so on, at the top of my voice. My heart raced as I gasped for air. I clutched the handles harder to make sure. Why that was the first song that came to mind I don't know, but I made it to the next rest stop. Thank you, Molly. Rider safety is paramount and I should have been more aware before riding. With that in mind I sat inside to rest for half an hour and I fuelled my tank with two espressos and a naughty custard doughnut before heading on, with no further issues except the raw open road. *Let me be warm.*

I arrived at Camping El Cantone in the early evening. Situated halfway between Jimena and Albanchez de Mágina, about 110 km north of Granada, it was a small family-run campsite, with pitches on gravel separated by high hedges, and an on-site bar. I spent the evening watching *Prison Break* in Spanish with the owners.

For breakfast the generous campsite owners made me a panini and coffee, and I booked to stay another night to enjoy the stunning day. It was mid-October at this point, and I had to pick Tash up in two days. The ride to Málaga was about five hours, no stopping, on the scenic route. There was time.

Jimmy-less, I walked the dirt track wearing shorts and T-shirt for the first time, in the opposite direction from arrival. Such a change in climate. It could've been summer. High-wired fences surrounded each property, to keep people out and dogs in. Two doors down, I met Rocco. We were friends for the day as we walked towards Albanchez de Mágina and the Hollywood-like sign on the mountainside. *He has a collar but why is he on the track?* I couldn't knock on the front door of these houses to ask if they were missing a dog. No buzzer to speak through either. *How do they get their post?* Large fences marked the edge of territory and the gates were locked; behind them were ferocious-sounding dogs. Not a chance I'd be venturing closer to the gates, let alone going inside. They were all quite terrifying when caught by surprise.

Thousands of olive trees spanned around as I came out into a field, gritty dirt underfoot. I reached a road and followed it the rest of the way, Rocco calmly at my heels. He was just big enough not to be a shit dog (definition: any dog small enough to be a rat).

As we approached the village, Rocco shot off without saying goodbye to follow a lady carrying a shopping bag. Disheartened by his lack of loyalty, I stopped in a café on the small square and soon forgave him over a coffee. The only spare seat outside was next to a grey-haired chap who, very relaxed, looked as though he'd been sat there for a century, carved out of stone. Shock, I was given olives as a free warm-up before the ham and tomato baguette. I offered the centenarian an olive. He declined. He's probably been eating them for years. Sick of them by now, I bet. A group of eight younger locals sat outside as they drank beers and smoked straight cigarettes at midday on a Wednesday. I could get used to this place! Every passer-by stopped for a chat with them. Some pulled up a chair and ordered from the busy owner, who was scuttling around catering for everyone's needs without breaking a sweat. A Land Rover pulled up. The driver leant out of the window and appeared to crack a joke to the crowd. Smiles all around. It was no bother to him that there were four cars held up behind him honking their horns. He moved with reluctance and parked down the road, then came to join them for a beer.

High on the mountain above the white sign stood a castle: Castillo de Albanchez. I went up the multicoloured steps in the village, around the corner from the main square. At the top of the steps were Tetris-placed houses, all with plastic bottles outside. It was unfathomable. I couldn't understand why they were there. There was a church with a water fountain in the courtyard, where apples bobbed around atop the water as pennies glistened below. Shit dogs barked through their windows. I didn't find the main path to the castle and was reluctant to walk back down the steps. I followed an animal-trodden path up above the houses and onto a cliff edge. The culprits of the trodden path were goats. *Now this feels like Cheddar Gorge.* I followed them from a distance, hoping they'd lead me the right way. The church below sounded its bell for 1 p.m. About thirty seconds later another bell in the distance went off.

It was like being in *The Lord of the Rings*, a childhood dream. Scaling rocks, under branches, navigating my way to the great tower. Samwise Gamgee over Frodo any day. I reached the top of the rock then scrambled down the slippery side to reach the proper path. The castle was a truly worthwhile visit – a mirador (lookout) with incredible views. Images on an information board portrayed how a battle would have taken place on the stronghold. The nooks and crannies of this compact castle can be explored if you're up for squeezing through the doors. I climbed on top of the flat roof and rolled a cigarette. Places like this warrant moments of reflection. Mount Kosciuszko in

Australia, Ben Nevis, Scafell Pike, Pen y Fan, the Lake District, skiing in the Alps and Austria, Crook Peak … all celebrated at the top. Only this time, I'd gone and left my lighter at the café. *Bugger.* Sufficiently soaked in views, I bounced down the main path back to town.

A different bar invited me in for a swift frothy one, and on the TV the news showed riots happening in Barcelona. I was relieved to have missed that one as there were "more than 500,000 people in protest at the heavy sentences handed down to Catalan politicians and activists".[2]

Rocco sat outside panting, having been on his own adventure. I found a communal water fountain so we both could drink before the long four kilometres back to camp in the heat. I questioned as we got closer to camp: *What am I going to do with Rocco?* There wasn't much I could do. He hung around for hours. He wasn't a stray. I couldn't have taken him with me on the bike; Jimmy would have been furious. Who was this furry companion I'd brought home? Maybe I should have walked around the block until he found someone carrying food to follow. At one point, which I felt terrible about, I picked him up and took him outside the barrier, but he just followed me back in. While my back was turned, he'd swiped my wooden cooking spoon and went to town on it. After a while he wandered off. I soon heard one of the long-term caravanners shooing him away with considerably more force than I had. Then he came back again!

---

2   https://www.theguardian.com/world/2019/oct/18/catalonia-general-strike-protests-independence

notes

- I later researched that those bottles of water are left outside the front of houses as a deterrent and to make cleaning up stray animal mess much easier. I'm unsure on the validity of this but I don't have a better reason
- Rocco definitely wasn't a stray, otherwise I'd have been more inclined to help him out. No way was Jimmy giving up his seat

I was a bit gutted when I woke. He was gone. I told myself it was for the best. I packed up, with Jimmy smug to be the sole furry friend of the trip. I headed for Granada on the A-401. The road paved its way through familiar olive farms, with the occasional rough road patches to avoid.

I swung into the outskirts of Granada for a wooden spoon and a shaver. What with Tash arriving, I supposed I had to clean up my scruffy fluffy beard and find some jeans that weren't padded or tracksuit bottoms, considering we'd be going on nights out on her week-long holiday.

On park4night I located a campsite by a reservoir about halfway between Granada and Málaga on the back roads. Avoiding the motorways in that area made for a much more interesting ride, albeit significantly longer, but as you probably know that's part and parcel. The views changed from crumbly fields to olive rows to fresh blooming hilltops emerging out of little villages. The campsite I found online was closed. Scratching my head, I was sure there would be somewhere remote nearby. Lo and behold I followed a dirt track which went down to the waterfront. A perfect spot in some well-spaced trees, not to be seen from the roads or the sky. You never know if they'll send the chopper out.

I could see right out across the reservoir. Pantano de Los Bermejales was the name of the place. There was a rented van parked up nearby with the same idea, belonging to an Israeli couple who were driving up to Madrid to then fly home. After some smiles and intros, they invited me for dinner: a simply superb rice and soya-chunk curry packed with flavour I didn't know could be achieved on a camp stove. It won't surprise you that we drank wine and spoke of the differences in culture, long after darkness fell.

They said two months was a long time to spend on my own in a tent. I completely agreed. It was far too long to be enjoying the fruits of the holiday's indulgence allowance. *Or was it?* It was too long to leave my partner at home, which is what they were implying. My only appointment of the whole trip happened to be the following day – picking up Tasha from the airport for a week.

I told them of how we met, one fun-fuelled Friday night at Glastonbury Festival in 2016, where in usual fashion, I wore my festival-stained white suit, face painted and Jimmy slung over my back. Tasha was head to toe in glitter and we danced until the morning to Rocket Lounge Jazz in the stimulating Shangri-La corner. The following Glastonbury was a different dance altogether (but that's another story!)

Before leaving the next morning, I warned the couple of the cold as they drove north, and advised them to pick up some warmer clothes in Granada as they huddled together under a thin blanket. Fires were still illegal in Spain that time of the year.

I'd booked us an Airbnb near Málaga for the Friday night, as she arrived at the airport at around 11 p.m. (I would not have been in Tasha's good books if I'd made her sleep in a tent that first night.)

I took the A-338 which led to the A-402, then made a scenic detour before rejoining the A-402. It was a beauty. I came out over a series of dipping roads before dropping into what felt like a giant pit. The flat land was covered in farmer's fields. Animals, crops and barns spread far and wide, confined by hillsides in every direction. In the distance ahead was an opening. A large natural gate. A parting in the rocks. The farms turned into the bustling streets of Ventas de Zafarraya with buildings on either side. People stepped onto the road without looking, with passing traffic going slow enough to stop. My eyes were fixated on the stone archway gate that loomed down on me. I passed through, and it was the heat that hit me before the scenery changed. I could see the sea! "I can see the sea!" I shouted to Jimmy, winning that game. *I must bring Tasha back this way.* I pulled in to marvel at the backdrop. A valley had formed its way through, with scattered houses and tracks all the way down to the sea. The road hugged the hillside on the right, which disappeared in parts then revealed itself again. The sea was still twenty-two kilometres away as the crow flies.

Part way down, I turned off into a gravel area to put last night's bottle in the recycling bin. In a lapse of concentration,

I pulled up alongside the slope and got off the bike. The stand was not fully down. In a second, the Shadow lurched forward and almost trapped my leg as I tumbled over with it onto the verge by the bins, face in the dirt. For a moment I lay in embarrassment, before calling to action. I rolled over and picked the bike up onto its side stand. I dusted myself off, feeling like a fool. Jimmy was also unharmed. As I examined the bike, the left foot pedal had taken the full brunt of the weight. There it lay on the ground, snapped clean off. The underside of it was severely scratched from my ability to oversteer on corners. A little knob of it remained on the injured Shadow, just enough to rest my boot and still be able to work the gears. Without much choice, I rode on.

One cramped foot later in Velez Málaga, I sought out a motorbike garage for a replacement or fixing. At the second garage, for a reasonable €15, they added a new fixing and did a bit of welding. I was out in half an hour. Good as new! The mechanic took a shine to Jimmy which helped in the transaction.

I arrived at the Airbnb with time to visit the launderette, wash, shave, eat and observe the tanned, wrinkled pieces of leather wander the pavements. I awaited Tasha's arrival.

A whole different adventure was about to commence.

notes
- thanks, India, for the introduction

15
THE CHICAS

Jim and the Chicas. We were like Charlie's Angels as the ladies led the show. We did without the sexist jokes, and instead of a wealthy powerful man dictating, there was me in the background carrying three bags full. We visited two great friends, Inma and Carmen, who lived with Tasha in Bristol. We met them in

Granada for the first weekend and again the following week at their family home in Almería. The last month alone on the road had been awesome. Nevertheless, this was a welcome change of scenery and together we made a formidable team.

Jimmy moved round to the back of the bike and I rejigged my luggage to accommodate Tasha and her carry-on rucksack. She rocked up from the flight complete with walking boots, padded jeans, helmet, and her motorbike jacket stashed with socks and shirts in the lining. Not your typical arrival wear that descends on the Bristol to Málaga flight each year.

The following day we checked out of our B&B and rode back up the A-402 which I'd been on the day before, and stopped for coffee at Restaurante Fuente La Peña. The smile on Tasha's face could not be wiped off. A lovely little place with outside seating and views to the valley that led to the sea. Inside, cured meat hung above the bar and a grill lay open by the entrance, shuttling smells throughout the restaurant.

"Turn around!" I shouted back to her as we reached the natural gates of Zafarraya, knowing the scenery behind was epic. As we passed the airport a couple of hours later, through the many swelling fields of olive trees, I recognised some of the larger engineering companies from my previous work and thought *I wouldn't have minded having a "work" meeting here.*

Tash had booked a homely, charismatic Airbnb in a cave house on a hillside in Granada, looking out onto the Sierra Nevada and the Alhambra, which was considerably cheaper than any central options. Plus, we had a laugh looking for it. The address was typed into the online map, and we neared the narrow stony streets, wide enough only for walkers and bikes.

I turned up a steep gradient track with loose sand and stones. At this point the commitment had been made. I couldn't have turned us around if we'd wanted to. I accelerated past the protruding rocks, leaving a dust cloud behind, knowing full well it wasn't the right way. *Oh my days, the views!* It was late afternoon and the sun still shone in the cloudless sky. The city sat calmly between the foothills of Sierra Nevada on one side and smaller hillsides on the other. I could picture the historic invasions taking place. We took five minutes to soak in the view and locate our accommodation, which we determined was a short walk down a path, but back around for the Shadow. As we sat on the ground and smoked a cigarette, squinting in the sun, a man appeared out of nowhere and stood opposite; an opaque figure, featureless thanks to the blinding light behind him.

"Quieres marihuana?"

I was taken a bit by surprise by this offer of cannabis. We'd not been there five minutes.

"Where are you from?" he asked.

"England," I replied.

In a deep accent, he said, "Ah, welcome to Granada. I've been here ten years. Welcome!"

We said our thanks and off he went downhill, in the same swift way that he had appeared.

Tasha pranced to the accommodation following the online map as I descended back down the steep, dusty path. I stayed in first gear which, although not good for the bike, saved putting on the brakes and sliding out. Towards the steeper bottom end, naturally we quickened, only just clinging on. I applied the brakes with full force, my feet down as stabilisers. I had to. If it weren't for the large groove and a rock to plant my front wheel into, I would have bailed, with the bike close behind. And if Tasha had been wriggling around on the back like she does, it was guaranteed. Clear of the sand and onto the safety of stone, I stopped to regather my breath.

On the narrow streets to our cave, a soft-top Mini had misjudged its width and almost took off its wing mirrors. The only available route was to reverse the forty metres backwards, towards me. I pulled in and waited on the top of downward-sloping steps. It was a long wait. You'd have thought they were reversing a trailer on sand. Catchy Arabic music blasted out of windows facing the streets, providing entertainment. Tasha appeared in view on the other side of the Mini, blocked from access. With hand-waving, pogo jumping and beaming smiles we bopped to the Moorish beats.

We spent Saturday night and Sunday catching up with Carmen and Inma, who toured us around the best parts of the city. Mainly the bars that offered the best tapas with your drinks. I lost count of how many we had, but we didn't need to go out for dinner. We just drank more beer!

We enjoyed walking the renowned "Sad Walk" to and from our accommodation. The markets were beautiful and there were often musicians and jewellery sellers, creating a welcome atmosphere that followed the stream down in the middle of the valley.

notes

- **the Alhambra** is a must-see, but purchase your tickets a month in advance as we didn't get to go inside. It's a hilltop fortress dated back to when the south of Spain was taken over by the Moors, a North African army. Built between 1238 and 1358

- a gentle meander around the city is the best way to see it. A mix of Spanish and Arab flavours fill the streets and food is free with your drinks in the old-school bars. Be sure to locate the smaller ones off the main streets as the larger venues tend to charge more for the ease of access and food
- tapas are included with the cost of the drink in Andalucía, the southernmost region of Spain
- thermal springs are a popular activity. We investigated some and paid to use a pool. Seemingly like everything we choose to do, we were surrounded by elderly couples. The water in the outside pool was warmish, but the highlight was a quick look at the Alhama de Granada spa: an Arab bath dating from the twelfth century and still toasty

After the weekend we made our way back to Torremolinos on the coast for a couple of nights before heading west to Ronda. Tasha was in charge of the week's schedule as it was her holiday. I was just her personal taxi driver.

notes

- no comments to provide on Torremolinos. It just had the only campsite open that we could find at the time. Ronda, however, is a must-visit

The ride from Málaga to Ronda contained long, flowing bends on reasonable roads. The town itself was truly impressive. The old town met the new on the Puente Nuevo bridge over Cascada de Ronda (Ronda Waterfall), where we wandered around for the day. We stumbled upon the Plaza de Toros de Ronda, which showcased Ronda's bullfighting history. *Can you condone animal cruelty for sport and still eat meat?* We opted not to go in but instead walked the wall ruins, made frequent wine stops, and admired the views and the bridge – more than enough to captivate us for a day, possibly two. We sat for a few hours below the bridge, sharing a large beer as the sun settled. As we left, I lost Tasha momentarily as she stacked her own cairn. The sound of a chainsaw in the distance was the only disturbance, and as ever, the power lines lay in view.

When dark fell, we stopped in a flamenco bar where behind a closed black curtain a show was underway. The barman said they'd had a couple of reservations not turn up, if we'd be interested. The show had been on for half an hour so we respectfully declined but stayed for a wine each. We peered through the curtains on the way to the bathroom and there were ten people in a room for fifty. That's a lot of reservations not to turn up. No doubt they would be packed in the summer.

notes
- there are many cheap beer and food options off the main stops. Weave your way through the tourists to find them. A highly recommended place to visit

After all these wonderful activities, the highlight of the night was watching two men carry a mattress down the street at 10 p.m. One dropped it, then picked it up, as the other dropped it, then picked it up. They both stood shouting, pointing and laying the blame on each other. It was like a scene from the Chuckle Brothers.

Once we'd returned back to the cold Airbnb room, full to the brim with food and wine, Tasha chirped up: "It won't take warm for the long to room up." We were both in stitches.

The next day we aimed for Almuñécar before continuing on to Almería. The A-7 was hard work on the bike. Fast, yes, but loud and relatively boring for both driver and pillion (passenger). The N-340 hugs the coast a bit tighter so we took this in parts, but it came with a significant increase in travel time. We stopped at La Herradura for a break to lie on the beach and get out of the leathers. The bay waters were calm and the beach stony but soft enough to walk on and lie down. I brought the magnetic tank bag onto the beach with the strap around my shoulder. It was a narrow beachfront and the bike was parked thirty metres from us and in view, so no problem with Jimmy on guard. A short nap and a swim later, we decided to grab a coffee before riding on. I placed the magnetic bag on the sparkling black paint of the tank, as I routinely do, only to be greeted with the screech of nails on a chalkboard. The magnets had picked up tiny stones from the beach and churned up the otherwise smooth black tank shine. I put a towel under the tank moving forward. Bloody magnetic stones and their stupid high iron content.

Spain's plastic sea covered every available space as we followed the weaving E-15. At first, we didn't know what they were. Since then, we've found they supply "about 3.5 million tons of fruit and vegetables annually to Europe's supermarket."[3] News reports have emerged from many corners over the years about the use of "African workers living in slums and working for less than half the legal minimum wage."[4] In addition, much of the waste is reported to be flushed out into the Mediterranean Sea.

We arrived in Almería after dusk, meeting Inma and family at their home in the city, and were welcomed to stay for the weekend. We met up with Carmen and her mum, Rosa, and were treated to a superb local meal out with fine wine, strong cheese, and sliced meat off the many hanging options. Sat around the kitchen table later, we conversed in Spanglish and laughed into the early hours.

On Saturday morning England beat New Zealand (19–7 FT) in the semi-final, during which I made all manner of noises before breakfast. Waiting for me to finish my excitable cheers, Carmen and her mum picked Inma, Tasha and me up to drive us around Almería for the day. We managed to fit in a multitude of experiences that we'd never have located on our own.

notes

- **El Mirador de la Amatista** or Viewpoint of the Amethyst. Our gorgeous guides pulled out a bottle of cava and nibbles as the Mediterranean Sea glistened beneath us in the beating sun. We ventured off to a smaller track and into the shrubbery as a large tourist bus swallowed up the viewpoint

3   https://www.dw.com/en/spains-sea-of-plastic-where-europe-gets-its-produce-migrants-get-exploited/a-47824476

4   Gary Wockner https://www.ecowatch.com/europes-dirty-little-secret-moroccan-slaves-and-a-sea-of-plastic-1882131257.html

- **Rodalquilar**. An eerie ghost village where there had been a gold mine. Gold was the last in a line of products to come out of the region, before the mines completely closed down in 1990
- **Playa del Arco**. Unique rock formations of eroded volcanic stone in intricate, peculiar patterns. A hotel and outdoor beach club nearby
- **the green hills of Almería**. Unrecognisable to the local eye due to the sheer amount of rain they'd had recently
- **La Isleta del Moro**. A quaint fishing hamlet with mouth-watering fresh fish and paella. Simply superb
- **Parque Natural del Cabo de Gata**. Wild flamingos gathered in the shallow waters. The beach nearby was perfect, the sand bright and the water clear as glass with silent surf
- **El Arrecife de las Sirenas** or The Mermaids Reef. We sat and watched the sunset at the lighthouse. Best one of the trip

Thank you for your hospitality and kindness. We had a truly magical time and it was hugely appreciated. Inma and parents Inma and Antonio; Antoñito and Abel; and Carmen and Rosa, see you all again soon.

On our way out we stopped in Tabernas Desert for a view of the Wild West wondrous wastelands, but mostly to see Texas Hollywood, home of popular Westerns including *The Good, The Bad and the Ugly*. With more time we may have paid to go in.

It was a long, blusterous and tiresome motorway stretch back to Málaga airport in time for Tasha's flight on Sunday night. Again that E-15 was not a pleasurable ride, and we really needed a screen at the front of the bike. Like driving your car down the M5 without the windscreen. Tasha almost nodded off after a week of slightly overboozing and little sleep. With not a great deal of time to spare, we pulled up and unloaded. We said goodbye with the usual three kisses and a bum squeeze. I'd be back in a month or so. And that was that. Tasha got her flight. My holiday from my holiday was over and I was back on the road. We'd had a sensational week and concluded that having scintillating friends for tour guides and transport were the key to success.

I almost ruined the week by crashing into the barrier leaving the airport car park. I had my wallet and throttle in the same hand, so I couldn't reach the brake as I slipped approaching the ticket machine, revving the engine unnecessarily, and jerked forward, reaching the clutch in time. I had to purposely stall to stop and catch my breath. My heart pounded. *You fool.* Unscathed, I made my way out. Jimmy resumed his normal position, pleased to have his rear seat back. I rode out into the night.

16
FREEDOM

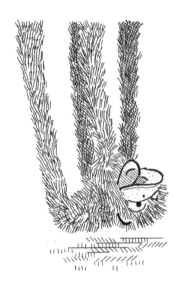

Maintenance.

I'd refused to go back to Torremolinos campsite, purely down to price, so I followed the A-404 west from the airport to Camping Málaga Monte Parc. It was cheaper and spacious enough, with a little shop and a bookshelf. I swapped *Cider with*

Rosie for another, which shall not be named as it wasn't worth reading. The campsite was by the base of Pino del Puerto de la Grajas (or Jarapalos), essentially a tree-covered mountain. I spent the day hiking off the beaten track after first crossing a busy road. I found an intact straw hat on the side of the road which proved useful on the hot day. The band read: "Autgestionem Cultura". Translation: "Self-Management Culture". Not great self-management from whoever lost it off their head as they drove past.

There were remarkable views at the top of Jarapalos. I'd reached the end of the water bottle ready for the fortunate arrival of a natural water fountain halfway up, encased in a giant stone bathtub. There were interesting remains of a kiln used to convert limestone into lime before cement was invented. A large square pool of water and a drainage system sat below, not worth the dip at the time as light was fading. I needed to get back to camp while I could still see the way.

After an early night I left at midday. There was a fast-food restaurant down the road that I used for the free Wi-Fi. I ordered an ice cream cone then a cheeky cheeseburger. In that order. I located a reputable garage in Torremolinos for a full service and two new tyres, which were much needed at this point in the trip. As the tyres were looking pretty bare I managed to book it in for the following day, which gave me another night to spend in the local area.

Again, I refused the Torremolinos campsite and I'm unsure why I didn't go back to Monte Parc. It wasn't that far away and would have had space, but there we go; these things don't always come to mind. Pinar de los Manantiales (Pine Forest of the Springs) came up in park4night, which recommended it was possible for campervans out of season but not for tents. To remain discreet, I didn't use one. The park was large and covered in scattered pine trees, as you'd expect from the name. A white church sat in the carved opening just off the middle, and swaying banks of raised ground and roots staggered the park surface. The odd concrete table was tucked away but welcoming. Ample room for many people. One was occupied by a family BBQ, and a couple of other cars lay scattered around like dice on a craps table. I'd arrived there late afternoon as the sun was thinking about settling down. The search for viable spots began instantly.

Topped up from the shop with a large beer and an easy dinner of chorizo, cheese, baguette, fruit and an extra-large packet of crisps, I was set for the night. I rode up into the woods and found a spot next to a tree, visible in the daytime from most places but not at night. At night it was too dark, pitch-black, out the way. Next to the bike I unfolded my ground sheet and laid it down, followed by my sleeping bag, then the second one. As Jimmy opted to stay on the bike and safeguard, I didn't get everything out. To my benefit no roof was required as the stars were out in force.

A short, still, somewhat surprisingly solid sleep.

Piercing through the pines, the sun reflected off the chrome shine of the forks. I turned my head towards the tree to avoid the morning light but rose shortly after. If the sun could reach me then I was visible to whoever would pull up in the park, so I packed up swiftly, then rode out for breakfast at a nearby café. The outside seats were busy with commuters on their way to work, although it wasn't as entertaining as watching people on the ferry. Early risers set out on their days in different fashion for the warm morning, from tight top buttons to cycle shorts and laptop bags. For a moment there I forgot people had day jobs.

I stopped by the garage mid-morning. Bike-free for a few hours, I headed to the beach in shorts and flip flops for the first time. Ridiculous. In five minutes of swimming, without intention, I picked up ten pieces of floating plastic and brought them ashore. It was shocking. We've always been mindful of the amount of plastic used and picked up litter where possible, but I'd not experienced that volume in the sea itself.

I made my exit and settled my fate by walking into a tourist-trap bar on the beach. The reasonable option of a ham and cheese toastie and a small beer was worth the coin. It was pointless trying to speak Spanish to the Dutch-speaking Dutch owners at the Dutch bar. A particularly touristy area of Spain, it seemed. A jogger stopped to chat with the owner.

"Long time no see! How are you?" the owner asked.

British bronze-coated Brian has lived on the beach there for twenty years but has had enough. Brian recently bought some land and a second house further down the coast because Brian fancied a change. Brian has a tough life.

I picked up Jimmy and the bike from the garage at about 1 p.m. Either as a gesture or because it was all they had, they'd hooked me up with larger tyres, which gave better cornering. It felt like I was dropping the bike every time I put it on the side stand, which took some getting used to. A damaging €450 later, I was on my way. They wouldn't expect me to be a returning customer.

notes

- use less plastic
- speak up more in fighting plastic pollution

Jimmy and me in Bourdeaux,
Chapter 6

A still image from the Le Puy-en-Velay light
show. Chapter 4

A cyclist at Mount Ventoux summit.
Chapter 7

Viaduc de Millau bridge.
Chapter 8

Parked by the River Tarn in Saint-Rome-de-Tarn.
Chapter 8

Camping spot by Montserrat.
Chapter 12

Castillo de Zafra.
Chapter 13

Jim, Tasha, Carmen and Inma in Granada
overlooking the Alhambra. Chapter 15

Viewpoint of the Amethyst, Almeria. (left to right) Tasha, Rosa, Carmen and Inma. Chapter 15

The touring party at the Mermaids Reef, Almeria. Chapter 15

The den at Fura Punta Carbonera beach. Chapter 17

Sat by the Shadow in Pinar de los Manantiales. Chapter 16

Benagil Caves.
Chapter 23

Entrance to Peniche Fortress.
Chapter 25

On the N222 through the Douro Valley, Portugal.
Chapter 26

In Vega de Gordón on the N-630.
Chapter 29

17
THE ROCK

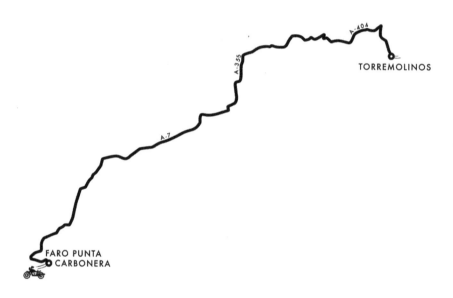

TORREMOLINOS

FARO PUNTA
CARBONERA

I followed the A-7 coastal road down towards Gibraltar. As I
passed a service café on the wooded roadside, I glanced towards
the coast. Glorious scenes with rocky partings in the trees and
glimpses of glistening sea. Then a small, white-walled settlement
– tough to say what size when travelling at speed – was all that

protruded from the hillside. I felt like a teenager walking past a mirror and noticing a large whitehead sitting high and mighty on the cheek, refusing to budge.

I reached Estepona and a Lidl stop, the only available option for food, before hunting for a wild spot on park4night as the surroundings were built-up. I followed the given route and entered a huge golf complex through security barriers. *Surely not.* Without question I was allowed through, past extravagant, fenced houses as golf buggies whizzed about.

I turned off onto a sandy beach track which came out at Punta Carbonera: a lighthouse. Dilapidated Civil Guard barracks and a bunker lay nearby. I continued down the dirt track without stopping, ending up by a motorhome that was parked up facing the beach. A dog ran out to greet me in the typical, overzealous way dogs do, tailing the bike as I rode at a crawling pace through the strong sea gust, the owner calling out behind me.

South African Graham and his family have been going there for years and assured me they'd not had any issues with the Civil Guard. I decided I'd set up camp a bit later, just in case, and left Jimmy basking in the breeze. With the Rugby World Cup final happening that coming weekend between South Africa and England, we discussed this at great length almost instantly. We both decided that based on form, England would take it, although he'd never have admitted it back in SA. (Graham is a fictional name created to protect his identity because of his statement.)

After thirty minutes of rugby chat we went our own way, and I headed down to the beach, armed with a blanket, wine, pistachios and dinner to cook. I smoked a cigarette as I pondered on the night's accommodation. A curious rock poked out of the water as the waves gently lapped around it, like a giant turtle head. Which reminded me of being caught short the previous morning, post-coffee in the pine park and knocking on the church door with no answer, which forced me to scrabble to a café down the road. (One of the main shortfalls of being on the road is the lack of certainty when it comes to actual bathrooms and the frequent nature pee stops.)

Massive tankers formed an orderly queue heading to Gibraltar port. The gert (south-west slang for large or great) rock stood clearly on the edge of land and sea. Ceuta, in Morocco, was just barely visible across the plain. The red sky dropped like a blanket thrown over a market stall as my rice in a bag started to boil in the pan. It looked like one of those empty bags I pulled out of the sea at Torremolinos earlier in the day. *I won't be using those again.* I flicked a pistachio shell in the direction of the dog poo a couple of metres away disguised as shrubbery, which I didn't spot when I first sat down. Half the shell landed on it like beach boules, and I lost the other half. I added a tin of tuna to the rice and feeling ravenous, I proceeded to dine without spotting another bit of plastic lodged in the tuna until it was part way down my throat. I didn't expect to find plastic waste in there!

Sat down closer to the water, I watched the lights appear on the Rock of Gibraltar. Behind me, the crescent moon was positioned perfectly above the working lighthouse, competing for brightness. My little finger fitted perfectly between the two.

The last notebook entry was written in the dark and after most of a bottle of wine. As such I have no clue what it said. Completely illegible.

I didn't have the energy to unearth the tent when I returned to the bike, so out came the groundsheet. I fashioned the larger one over the top of the bike to form a part shelter, with large logs holding it down to the ground as the pegs weren't complying. There was enough room to crawl into my sleeping bag. I could have put the tent up in the time it took me to build the den, but it would have been much less fun. I found the other half of the pistachio in my shirt top pocket before I drifted off.

Three keen fishers arrived at the crack of dawn. Another car pulled up soon after, closer to my bike than the others, which forced me to leave my moto den in a groggy state. The latter arrival was a shallow spear fisher, kitted up with camouflage wetsuit, flippers and floating device, and a speargun that hung down by his side. I wished him good luck as he headed towards the sea: "Buena Suerte." He turned and waved back, smiling. It's the little things.

Before leaving, I donated our Monopoly Deal set of cards to Graham and family. Tasha and I loved playing it, but it's no good on your own. His kids would enjoy it and it saved me some space. Although neither of us meant it, we wished each other good luck in the Rugby World Cup final before I left for Gibraltar through the golf security barriers. A buggy chase was potentially afoot.

18
TARIFA PIRATES

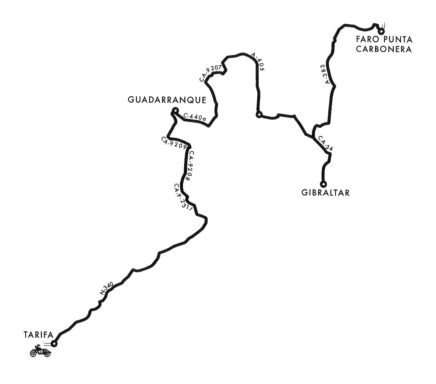

Before border patrol I delved deep inside my tank bag to locate my passport. I'd taken my gloves off in the process and wedged them into the side pocket of my jacket while I dealt with the checks. The border patrol man stood blocking the way, handing over my passport to the booth with an impertinent look. By the time he turned back to me with my passport he was wide-eyed with a welcoming grin, waving me through to merge onto an airport runway. A bit taken aback, I stopped to think for just a second, before the loud horn behind ushered the belief it was the right route. Feeling flustered from the horn I rode barehanded into Gibraltar. I looked for a place to stop to glove up, settling on a small car park. Routing around in my jacket, I found only one. I was sure I'd put it in my pocket. It didn't seem worth returning through the runway at the time, as the entry was a stressful experience. *I'll ask on my way out.* I cut my losses and dug around in the panniers for the spare pair I knew I'd brought for the ride.

Shortly after arrival I was ready to leave Gibraltar. Granted, there were some interesting streets and a decent breakfast at Europa Point Café, plus the new Gibraltar rugby stadium right on the coast – part-built but impressive – yet it wasn't a destination I wanted to spend any real time in. I stood out on the point's edge, hanging on the whisper that there may be whales visible. Not that day.

With no pull-in back at border control to ask about my missing glove, I begrudgingly added it to the lost items list and rode out in my spare pair. I should have bought fuel, cigarettes and a bottle of tipple from that side of the border as it would have saved me a few quid.

Opting for the back roads out of Gibraltar, I pulled into a small village bar for a beer and an espresso, which is where I met Brummie Bill. He was a lone wolf sat outside in the latest Brit holidaymaker fashion, directing me to park on the pavement.

"It's no bother to park there," he said after I switched off the engine.

After sitting down outside with a bottle of lager, at his request, I told him about my trip. I mentioned Somerset and this set him off on a cider-fuelled memory in his thick Brummie accent.

"I used to cycle four miles to the cider house when I was a young 'un. Ol' Marvey Tuck used to have a large wooden barrel of cider and hanging bacon. He cut a slice this thick and would toss it into the pan. Those were the days. Of course, got gout now and cider's 'bout the worst for it. Shame. Got to drink this piss now," he said as he picked up his bottle of lager. *Which I'm sure is worse!* Short, stout and full of gout.

I hit rain in the hills above Tarifa. Rather, the rain hit me. On went my useless waterproofs. It was too late for Jimmy, the sodden mess. Ten minutes later I descended from the hills and arrived in Tarifa to bright sunshine ricocheting off the old town walls and the sapphire blue of the ocean with ticks of white waves.

A Dutch licence-plated motorbike led me through town, which I thought I'd follow for a bit. They led me straight to my hostel. It was decent for €13 a night. Cheaper than some of the campsites!

notes

- South Hostel, I would recommend. Kitesurfing rental and lessons available. Tarifa is one of the best spots in the world for kitesurfing. The Mediterranean meets the Atlantic, so take your pick, warm or cold
- beautiful views of Morocco on a clear day

- being the most southerly point of Spain, lots of travellers seem to wait out the winter there

I didn't even realise it was Halloween until I walked into town. Most of the cafés and shops were closing with the bars coming to life. Kids were dancing on a stage in the square to Michael Jackson's "Thriller". I sat and had a beer while watching the show, reminiscing about school plays and pantomimes.

Down by the harbour was Bar La Burla. Small and intimate with good service, free Wi-Fi, great music choice, and tapas on tap. I admired a skull-over-crossed-surfboards badge that read "Tarifa Pirates", sewed onto the rucksack of a customer, which turned out to be an adventure sports clothing store.

On a rare occasion I would watch a film on my phone in bed. This time, around midnight. Two lads who had just turned up in the dormitory said hello. They asked if I could move my bike forward two feet so they could park their car outside. I didn't reply for a few moments as I considered my options:

1. I'm asleep.
2. No, sorry.
3. As I'm awake I suppose I could.

Out the front there was acres of room for their two-door fancy Audi A3. I could've parked it for them but didn't mention it. I wheeled my bike forward then relocked the hefty chain. Back to bed. Two different lads returned in the early hours from Halloween drinks. Double trouble. *Brilliant.* I felt like a grumpy old man.

New Zealand beat Wales in the third-place play-off (40–17 FT) which I watched on my phone, eating my scrambled eggs in the hostel kitchen. I considered returning to Gibraltar to watch the Rugby World Cup final with some atmosphere. Looking at the price of accommodation, though, it was expensive, and I didn't want to retrace my steps that far. As I booked night by night, I had to change rooms at the hostel. I planned to rent a windsurf set or get a kitesurfing lesson. It wasn't to be.

I sat up on the roof of the hostel that evening reading and considering the next options. *What's stopping me getting the ferry to Africa?* Oh yes, Tasha set me a travel time limit that was reaching its end. Enthusiastic American Danny came up on the roof and offered me a cigarette. We sat and talked for a while; or rather, I sat while he stretched. He was an interesting character, hitchhiking through Spain, putting his Spanish language to good use, sleeping in his hammock in the bushes and offering to volunteer at local communities with his experience in projects and marketing – or something like that. Entertainingly, there were a noticeable number of "dudes" and "bros" that were thrown out every other word.

Ten minutes after his exit, I went down the stairs. Quite literally. The stairwell was pitch-black and I couldn't see my way. I felt out for the walls before stepping. I thought the five steps were three. I stepped off, expecting to reach the landing. My right foot caught the edge of the bottom step. I hit the deck hard on my side. My ankle twisted. Pain surged around the joint. It was agony. As I lay on the floor, motionless, the motion light came on. *A bit feckin' late!*

I hopped to my room and onto my bed, and told myself that I'd done it numerous times in rugby before and it would fix itself soon enough. I informed reception about their dodgy light and booked a couple more nights to be sure it would heal. I couldn't walk, let alone ride. As a common victim of chocolate ankle syndrome (easily snappable), this was a feeling I was all too familiar with; the joint was perplexed as it palpitated, laid out forlorn, risen on the bed.

Rugby World Cup final day. I was buzzing! England v South Africa (12–32 FT). I sat in the common room and watched the final on my phone with enthusiastic American Danny. We had a few mid-morning beers. Then a couple more beers after South Africa gave England a spanking. Losing was actually made easier by having to explain to Danny each aspect of the game.

Self-sorrow, resting my ankle and medicating took up the remainder of the day. I imagined South African Graham celebrating on the beach in his caravan. Congrats. Well deserved.

This led me to Sunday, and I was ready to leave. I left the hostel with no real destination set but the open road. The only way now was north.

A beach campsite appeared two minutes outside of Tarifa, and without thinking I turned in to book in for a night. This turned into two. Torre de la Peña. It was at a petrol station beforehand, the ankle pain having subsided whilst riding, that I planted my foot as I usually would when stopping, sending ripples of pain through my leg. More R & R needed.

The campsite reception was across the busy road, with low-hanging trees that hugged the thin strip of land between road and sea. A pedestrian tunnel ran under the road, just wide enough to take the bike through. The echoing roar of the engine in the tunnel turned heads as I popped out the other side like a cork from a bottle. The area for tents was well shaded, with plenty of places for Jimmy to hang out in the branches above.

Images of Olive Oyl and Popeye stared me down. They provided security services from up high on a ledge, judging those who entered through the toilet doors.

A cyclist called Sam was camped under a set of trees. He was about the same age as me and had real motivation to cycle a long way every day. We shared some stories. He'd cycled from Belgium and strained his wrist in doing so. Too many miles in too little time. He was held up in the camp searching for the best route home. What a pair of invalids we were. We chatted and laughed for hours over wine, well into the gathered darkness, the sea no longer visible but waves crashing all night long.

A lovely, relaxed sunny Monday by the beach. What a contrast to the typical Monday routine. The single downfall being there was no chance of windsurfing as my ankle still throbbed.

19
BARKING MAD

The next day Sam and I departed in opposite directions at midday, risking the 11 a.m. check-out. No issues ensued. Jimmy and I continued west into a natural reserve area. A few kilometres down a track was a cosy restaurant surrounded by well-off houses. It was a dead end but with lovely golden sands.

As I turned off the E-5 main road, this pristine sand was piled high on either side. It was like the parting of the Red Sea. In this rendition, sand represented the ocean and the crossing was roughly thirty metres. I was Moses, Jimmy was the Israelites, and God was a bright-red digger.

I rode back out and round to Bolonia. Nothing was open for food in the late afternoon and I ended up in another tiresome dead end. The campsite at Zahara de los Atunes was closed and I couldn't find a wild spot reachable by bike. I didn't feel up for riding a great distance, so I stopped just up the coast at Campo y Mar, on the road to Barbate.

A couple of polite German ladies sat outside their large motorhome, basking in the manageable afternoon heat. "The owners will be back soon," they assured me. I had considered leaving and trying the next place as I felt particularly impatient at the time. The owners returned from their shopping trip at the point I mounted the Shadow. Off I stepped to greet them.

The building was a brilliantly bright place for a campsite. Small in scale but high in walls that shielded campers (only Jimmy and me) from the coastal gales which had picked up. The owners were equally as intriguing as their venue. Distinctly welcoming. They'd packed up their belongings and left for Spain, aiming to run a campsite. *What a great idea!* Their choice was a classic discotheque venue from the nineties that had been collecting dust until they moved in. The dance floor and concrete bar areas still stood outside, and with the addition of artificial grass it was coming to life. Inside, a circular dance floor had been turned into a communal lounge and family space for people to use. A large white pillar stood in the middle of the room, holding up the ceiling. The animated mosaics on the floor still shined.

The beach around me was luscious sand, and to the north I caught sight of the dusty walls of Barbate, which was separated by an estuary opening, with sea walls to direct the water's flow. The combination worked well. It was easy on the eye. On the flip side, on the beach plastic was rife. I took out a bin bag and filled it. I could have been there all evening strolling the entire beach.

I stayed the following day and night due to the kind hospitality. I woke early for a cold morning swim before strolling to Barbate, walking over the bridge. The path followed the estuary edge through a park, on the walking and cycle lanes that flowed side by side. Small fishing boats lay stranded on the mud flats at low tide. The sound of laughter and a puny engine turned my head as two boys on a moped pulled a wheelie down the cycle track. Pretty impressive. Totally unconcerned by passers-by, their mates stood blocking the walkway further up, passing an extra-large cigarette between ten.

I sat for a beer outside in a café overlooking the beach. *Busy for a Wednesday.* The wind swept the sand across the empty plains, the whole ocean vacant except for a kid surfer on the receiving end of his father shouting from the shore. In the seating area young mothers gathered for cold drinks and cradled their children, whilst in contrast a disrespectful group of lads in flat peaks and baggy branded clothes jested blatantly about a waitress, slapping each other on the arms, trying to live up to their egos with little regard or respect for her feelings as she went about her job, ignoring them.

Leaving Barbate, I walked back onto the quiet beach that met the orange sky head-on. A motorboat out to sea sped silently as waves rose and fell into the shore. I put my headphones on. "Blowing in The Wind" by Bob Dylan was the first track to play. I sang as loud as my larynx would allow. A jogger passed and glanced back at me as I continued my tone-deaf singing as though he wasn't there. "Dance like there's nobody watching" is a quote I believe in.

If it were the middle of summer and I wasn't chasing the weather home, I would have stayed there and helped on the restoration work at the campsite. The longer I left it to head north, the colder it would be.

The following day, as I rode through the more central part of Barbate on my way out, small cafés spilled off the pavement into the streets, creating a great vibe. I sniffed out the fish district and then a little market row on the outskirts by the port. A strange town all in all, but I liked it.

Tasha had wanted to visit Cádiz but we didn't have time. Plus, the Shadow didn't have enough tread left in the tyres to risk it. I would head there with Jimmy and rub it in. I opted to search early for a campsite or wild venue, whichever came first, in commuting distance from Cádiz so I could visit the next morning. The rains came early so I promptly pulled in for lunch at a road restaurant. Sat under the outside shelter, I Cheddar gorged on a cheeseburger from a slim menu, with a beer and an espresso on the side. I enquired at the campsite opposite, but at €22 a night it wasn't a viable option for my cheap arse.

I arrived in El Palmar in that annoying light rain. Dreaded drizzle. It was a hip, beach-facing strip of surf hire and bars, most with shutters down. A hive of activity in the summer months, no doubt. Not far ahead, a side road opened up into a large, uneven grassy area outside a hotel, where two vans were parked up: a plain, rented camper and another bright blue and green supertruck with camels stencilled on the front. *Wicked.* It was an aged, patched-up Nissan Diesel with ample room. Storage popped out of both sides like a fire engine. As I sat in admiration, a pleasant Bulgarian man came out for a chat and advised that the police came often so it was not good for a tent, yet a self-sufficient van was fine. I wandered into the bushes anyway but found nothing but nappies and used toilet roll. Such a shitty shame.

I considered many spots on the coast. Under a power mast, behind a shipping yard, through bushy sand dunes, and yet another closed campsite. The area was quiet enough but the spots were not great. They posed a large chance of being foiled. I stopped at a security guard's booth at Roche and asked about a forest area that stood nearby. My question was practised but I couldn't understand his answer. I nodded, smiled and repeated, "Sí … Sí … Sí … Sí," in response to his answers, hanging on to every intonation he made in case it was a question directed at me. Fortunately not. Or at least I didn't respond to any.

I parked further up the road, out of sight from him, and wandered into the forest for a gander (not a male goose but a glance). I decided on a spot and a safe access route to minimise puncture risk. I started walking back through the wooded area to the bike. *Someone's revving a motorbike engine.* Quickly followed by: *Fuck! My bike!* I realised it was coming towards me at a rate of knots. I stopped and hid behind a tree, and peered through the woods for a glimpse of the oncoming machine. Some seconds later, a dirt bike came racing through the spot I'd chosen to put my tent – the bugger. It would've taken it and me out completely if I'd put it up already. Another spot, then.

I must head inland. The coast was too built-up. I found a natural park online, Pinar de la Dehesa de las Yeguas, with good reviews for walkers and runners, accompanied by a picture of a camper van. It had a large parking area that ran all the way through the centre, with dense pine forest and concrete benches either side. Footpaths weaselled their way through partings. Wooden barriers marked perimeters but one was broken, allowing just enough room for the bike to sneak through. I investigated on foot, although I'd already discovered there were no issues for the cruiser off-road. Once sure there were no witnesses, I rode across the line and into the bushes.

As I set up my tent, a dog walker wandered past and we exchanged a "Hola" and a wave of the hand. He was not bothered in the slightest by my hiding. I stayed put.

Night fell and dogs barked. There must have been a kennel nearby. Then a disconcerting scream came from inside the park. I'd heard before about foxes or birds or something of the sort making awful screaming sounds. I did wander down to see if my tent lights could be seen from the car park. I was hidden, safe out of view.

20
SUNNY CORLEONE

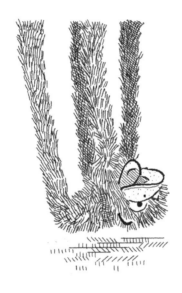

Early the next morning I took down the tent and sat on one of the benches in the park's centre clearing. It was a particularly fresh start, the sun creeping through the trees as the rays ricocheted off a gorgeous ginger and white cat. It wandered over for attention. It was the spitting image of a gangster-like feline friend we used to have in the family, Sunny Corleone, a tribute to Sonny. I'd been driving around Australia in my Land Cruiser at the time of his passing, yet only upon my return home some months later, when there was no answer to my shouts, did the penny drop that I hadn't been told.

A local walker stopped for a chat as coffee brewed on the concrete tabletop that had small graffiti tags scattered on the flat surface. "The cat – it's yours, from England?" he asked as he pointed to my GB sticker on the bike. We laughed together at the thought of the cat with a helmet on, scooting up next to Jimmy. The local didn't want a pan of coffee from the crazy man sleeping in the park, funnily enough.

I rode to Cádiz. A couple of coppers cruising on duty amorously leered at a woman walking by. There was a bus driver in Barcelona that shared their same slimy smile. I felt the need to apologise to all women who have endured being gawked at by dodgy blokes.

Torre Tavira was the first stop: a museum inside one of the one hundred and thirty-four watchtowers in the city. These "are witness to the trade and prosperity which the city experienced in the eighteenth century".[5] From the roof, there were defining 360-degree views on to the straight streets and squared rooftops below. Merchant ships entering would have been in clear view in the impressive seascape. The camera obscura, an optical device producing visual effects using light, delivered scheduled, manual presentations as part of the museum's programme. They dug deeper into the landmark parts of Cádiz. The wait was too

---

5   https://www.torretavira.com/en/tavira-towers-history/

long for the English talk so I joined the imminent Spanish session, comprehending very little but finding myself laughing along with fifteen other people standing in a circle around the device, albeit a split second behind.

Cádiz was an engrossing and alluring city. Men fished over the walls, and the cobbled one-way streets were narrow. An indoor fish market close to Torre Tavira packed its stands full of sand shark and live lobsters, and neighbouring stalls displayed fresh fruits and cured meats. A truly bustling venue, where all of the senses came into play. The vibrant colours on show were a spectacle in themselves and helped draw the crowds. Stallholders shouted deals and made eye contact with passers-by, proud to have their freshest produce on display. The flow of smells was a whirlwind of elusive treats, so I stood still to investigate the source and then followed my nose. Incredibly different to the local markets back home. I only wished I had a kitchen nearby or a fridge on my bike at the very least. Surely that's not too much ask?

In the southern part of the city I stopped at a beach bar for a quick beer and espresso. Captain Morgan himself sat on the table next to me, complete with hat, beard and all. Although I was the smellier pirate.

At a self-service car wash I gave the Shadow and Jimmy a power hose down after all the off-roading we'd been doing. Both were full of filth. Myself included, but I didn't fancy the force of the power hose. The natural park was a tried-and-tested spot so I returned there via a supermarket on the outskirts of Cádiz. There was a local bar next to the shop, which I thought could be fun times. I swung in for a small one – €1 a beer, the cheapest yet. Two half-cut locals clocked me as I walked in. Their expressions put me slightly on edge as I ordered. One turned and bumped into me, spilling my beer. Rather than kicking off, as I was half prepared for, solely on the basis of being a foreigner in a local boozer, he apologised profusely, and I smiled and lowered my guard, embarrassed to have thought otherwise. In hindsight, the looks they first gave me were more inquisitive than glowering. His mate came outside to where I sat, and rolled a cigarette.

"Lo siento por mi amigo. El es ..." he said, apologising for his friend and making the international crazy gesture with his finger. I tried to hold on to the conversation and stick with him. I think even if I spoke Spanish, I would have had a hard time understanding. As a fellow mumbler myself, I can say he'd fallen deep into that category. We shook hands many times, then, as I left, they made motorbike sounds with their mouths. Drunk, rosy cheeks vibrated as saliva rippled out, which made me chuckle and shudder simultaneously. Jimmy and I lapped back round on the bike to honk the horn before riding off, casting a wave to the locals of Cádiz.

The police arrived at the park that night and drove a lap. I was well enough hidden. I laid the tent on the ground; I'd finish putting it up later, just in case. I plugged in my headphones, opened a beer and danced outrageously in the opening by the tent, leaving my shuffled footprints in the fallen pine needles to "Dope VHS Master" by Desmond Cheese. If you haven't heard it, plug it in, close your eyes, and lose yourself. You're welcome.

It had been a cold and unpleasant night in the tent again. I felt lonely when I woke and I struggled to shake it. The pessimist in me struck a chord that I couldn't help but contemplate. As a result, a slow morning followed. I cradled my coffee from the comfort of my sleeping bag, my beanie hat was pulled down to my brow and I urged that fresh coffee scent into my nostrils. The four walls of the small tent aided my thoughts. *As soon as I step out that zipped nylon door, the optimist will stand up and action my day, one step at a time.* The quote "The optimism of the action is better than the pessimism of the thought" sprung to mind. It was on a picture that hung in the house I grew up in. From memory, I think it was taken from a New Internationalist article, but I can't be sure.

I committed to getting up, bursting for a piss. I hung my CamelBak water sack off a branch. Then, stood bollock-naked, I hosed myself down with the measly spout. The sun shining through a gap in the trees provided some warmth, but it still felt like a cold shower after a December day's amateur rugby match in the visitor showers of the opposing team. A chilly dribble came out the shower head and nowt to brag about.

On this occasion, and many others, as I packed up to move on I had to release the air in my mummy-shaped mattress before rolling it up. The cap flipped open which released my reeking dinner breath from the night before. Cheese scented mainly, with a hint of chorizo. *(Retches partially) I must remember to clean my teeth before blowing this up.* It never happened that way. Jerez (pronounced Hereth) was next, as a friend of my ma's lived and worked there. It was generous of her to put me up for two nights. I had not seen Viv since I was waist-high, smaller maybe, so it was nice to catch up. She showed me fantastic tapas and flamenco, and I heard a few stories that I didn't know about my mother. We went to a famous seafood restaurant with her friends, which served handfuls of lightly battered assortments. The Sunday flea market made for interesting viewing and I picked up a woolly jumper. Not good for my eczema, but warmth became the priority.

notes

- sherry is produced locally in the Andalucían region, specifically Jerez. Granny's favourite is Harvey's Bristol Cream. Her garden is laden with the remnants of a lifetime of blue-bottled tipples, but the winery was closed Sunday and Monday, so no souvenir for the collection
- I'd most certainly visit Jerez again
- thanks for your hospitality, Viv. Great to see you again

21
RUBBISH COASTAL VIEWS

At a few sets of lights entering Seville, I would eye up a moped, urge them for a race, then always let them shoot off first to get the win. I'm sure Seville is great, but I wasn't after another city break.

I opted to head for the scenic coastal route again and followed the A-474 out of Seville, turning south into Parque Nacional de Doñana. I expected to see vast open space but found only large plots with high fences. Dotted villages appeared after stretches of straight, fast roads. Mushroom-shaped trees sat in ghostly squares as the main route trickled through town centres, then an unmarked road before the A-483 down to Matalascañas. The sight of burnt trees became ever more present – remnants of a 2017 bushfire. Campers with their gas stoves were often to blame. I took extra precautions each time to ensure that nothing flammable was in the impact radius if it were to topple over. Securing the base with rocks also worked.

I located a cliffside spot overlooking a beach bar. The views were wide, and it was a popular spot. Bags of rubbish and toilet rolls were littered everywhere. No wonder wild camping is illegal in most countries. The aftermath is revolting and downright disrespectful. I'm sure to leave only footprints on any stays.

Being agile on two wheels, I managed to find an unused spot well back from the cliff edge. Hedge hidden; if a patrol were to arrive they'd have had a hard time finding Jimmy, the Shadow and me. Before heading to set up camp, I spent the evening sat like a king looking out to sea. Jimmy hung on a branch above the bike, on lookout. No one came. November wasn't really the time for too many campers.

For the second time of the trip, I'd sat in an ant's nest. Also for the second time, I found one in my knickers.

Various-sized boats were making their way to Huelva port west of me. It was like a game of battleships played on a flipboard.

There were five ships: a five-piece carrier, two three-piece destroyers and two three-piece battleships. I might have missed one, I couldn't remember how many pieces there were. They sat roughly at G1 to J1, F6 to F7, and J3 to J4, and none sunk.

The sun had been dropping slowly, pushed down by a horizontal plate of clouds. The ruby shade grew deeper with each stretch. Ships still stood, having hardly moved. Lights started flickering out across the sea. Mostly white, but two flashed red and green. I couldn't tell if it was because of intoxication at this point and too much staring, or if a fishing operation was underway. I rubbed my eyes again and again. They were still there. I pulled out my phone and took a video of complete darkness, only capturing my Darth Vader breathing.

I couldn't see the words I wrote as it was so dark. (This happened the drunk I more, yet I insisted on adding more notes to the blank pages. The later it got, the more illegible my writing became.) I went back to see Jimmy and set up the tent, aided by moonlight. I heard an owl and stopped to listen for a while, gently swaying. I thought I heard an owl at our camp at Glastonbury Festival one year as I lay on my back, head spinning, muddy boots outside the tent. It was a pigeon.

notes

- to save water, cook the broccoli before the couscous then reuse the water. If you're really short, it can be reused for coffee the following morning
- Battleships is a strategic game for two players, where you can't see the other player's ships on their board but have to try and sink them, by guessing one square at a time

First thing in the morning I rose without quarrel. Instantly, I sat on the remaining packet of couscous which proceeded to burst at the seams, sending grains to every crevice of its new-found spacious environment. In the clean-up I found my week-long-lost pink lighter in my sleeping bag. It fell out with the couscous as I shook it. I felt like the first sibling to get the toy out the new cereal box.

Avoiding eye contact with Jimmy, I had another nature CamelBak shower. I wasn't as short for water as I'd initially thought. There was no need to use the broccoli water for coffee that morning either, but I'd already committed to the pour. Stood on the cliff edge, I sipped my stimulating broccoli brew, watching the seagulls give the fishing boats havoc out to sea.

My last stop before Portugal was in one of the tourist towns close to the border: Isla Cristina, I think it was. I cruised the desolate streets past properties that lay empty on the beach front. Little signs of life or movement apart from the gently lapping waves at the edge of the sand. Garages were opened to see right through them, no doors at either end. Gardens lay lonely with no bucket, spade or bodyboard. No dogs barked. No one swam in the sea. Apartment blocks had no washing out on their balconies and the sun reflected off the closed white shutters rather than being absorbed by bathers. There was no waiting at junctions, roundabouts or fuel stations. Restaurants catered for eighty but only four seats occupied the waiter's attention. An out-of-season eerie send-off.

I sipped on the espresso and paid up. The buzz came as I stepped back on the bike with a spring (coffee) in my step. I was apprehensive about Portugal because I had done little research.

New place. New language. Are the fuel stations the same? Will they take cards? (Tasha brought me out my Visa!) Are campsites open? Is wild camping frowned upon or illegal, like in Spain? Are speed limits the same?

Those questions rattled through my head as I crossed the border bridge, avoiding eye contact with the police officers parked on the roadside, my sun visor being put to good use. I said adiós to Spain and released the Shadow beast.

22
PODENGO

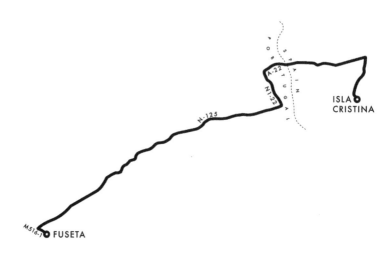

I have to go back through Spain to get the ferry, you doughnut, I thought as I turned off onto the N122 to follow the coastal road. Hasta luego – see you later – rather than adiós.

The first difference I noticed was the increase in Mercedes. Every other car was an old box-like Merc. Some had been lowered and had spinners, and most had a spoiler, like the Civics and Peugeots that would be souped-up back home, racing up and down the Gorge. Much cooler, though.

After I had followed the N125 for a short while, I stumbled upon a fenced, square campsite filled with long-term campers in Fuseta. The sea was in view from the front gate, separated by a car park, and there was a restaurant a bit further up. Somewhere to shower, fill up water bottles and sleep for the night. So started the Portuguese stretch.

Towards the main beach was a wooden walkway over a large marshy area, which led to a sandy beach island. A lifeboat hut perched on stilts was partially submerged by the quivering tide. Two paddlers shared the duty on one board, only their silhouettes visible. Another picturesque finish to the day.

Wait. Not for everybody.

A dog on the beach ten metres behind me shot off into the marshes. One of the two owners waded after it, cursing, before retreating to avoid sinking. A bird flew low over the marshes, the dog still in pursuit. I watched for the next ten minutes the owner whistled and begged the dog to come back. It did not. I left across the footbridge and was walking through the car park when the dog ran past. Potentially a Podengo, the national dog of Portugal. A strong, quick and handsome hound, medium-sized and covered in mud, still chasing something. The bird likely flew inland, so it had to lap back round some buildings. The Podengo ran past a few young kids as they tried to grab him. He showed no interest and bolted through. They couldn't have been any older than four. One lad ran off to chase the Podengo, leaving the other two behind. He gave up after ten metres, then, without turning around, he lifted up his towel to moon at his mates, who fell about laughing, and his mum ran over to pull his towel down. That kid has a bright future. Pure comedy genius. I was in hysterics.

The dog jogged by the campsite an hour later. Still muddy. Still ownerless.

At the campsite bar, just as I arrived a motorbike enthusiast was leaving. I could tell because of the Harley T-shirt, bandana, white camouflage trousers and leather waistcoat. Pretty obvious. He then proceeded to drive off laughing on a pink four-wheeled electric scooter. It was quite the picture.

The book that shall not be named was swapped out for *The Buddha of Brewer Street* by Michael Dobbs.

23
HAPPY BIRTHDAY

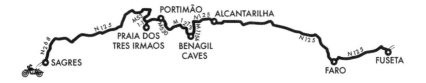

Tasha's birthday. November 13. Every year. A 6.30 a.m. wake-up call from nesting birds in the branches above was followed by a head-splitting cherry picker, chainsaw and chipper machine going to work on the campsite trees. A beatbox battle ensued between them. Regardless of the morning mixtape mash-up, the sky was clear and crisp. It looked like a great day.

To celebrate, in Tasha's absence, I took the day to see tourist sights in the area.

Not far down the road was the Chapel of Bones at Alcantarilha: a sixteenth-century building with an estimated five thousand human bones decorating the inside. It was a small chapel at the side of a church. Various-shaped bones lay on their side, filling the gaps between skulls. It was a rare, lonely place of reflection – apparently unusual for most of the bone chapels in Portugal as hordes of tourists visit each year. Memories of the Killing Fields in Cambodia and the skull towers flooded through. This was a great deal less heart-wrenching than those violent scenes. It felt more like artwork.

It was then a short distance to Benagil caves (Algar de Benagil), right on the coast, for a more light-hearted activity.

For twenty euros I rented a paddleboard instead of taking the more expensive boat tour. The access point was from the beach, Praia do Benagil. Jimmy was left parked on the pavement behind a small storage hut where they rented the boards, and next to a café. Steep steps went up to a fancier restaurant with bay views. Jimmy looked after everything as I stripped down ready for the water. The waves came in with decent force and dropped abruptly on the shore, so choosing the opportune moment to pick the gap was crucial. I made my way out. I stood up, paddled twice, wobbled on a wave, then crashed off, jarring my ankle in the process. The beach was packed with onlookers. I knew I would have laughed so was pleased to have provided some entertainment. Now on my knees, I paddled on.

Two entrances to the cave formed a dual arch, each facing out to sea. The tide flowed in sets, in and out. Like the beach, the waves dropped without warning. I rode the wave in like a bull, gripping onto the reins for my life; then, close to the sand, it threw me overboard and I hit the water, then the shore, with a thud. A pair in a double kayak came in after me. Dry up until that point, they were projected then capsized. Bags, sandals and paddles hurled through the air. They washed up on the sand like arriving on a desert island. I chuckled and helped them gather their things.

The cave was a mesmerising mouth, not deep with tunnels but open with circular indents in the rock. One had worked its way to the surface above, where little heads popped over from the viewing platform. The sides were the colour of honeycomb, small air pockets that formed life-cycle shapes. The M-shaped arches let in the light that glistened off the sea as the swell crashed around smaller rocks on the little beach. Watching people exit on boards was just as amusing as the entrance.

Drip-drying with a beer at the café, I observed the board man try to fish between rentals. Like a yoyo he put the rod down to serve another customer. Then another. And another. At long last he managed to cast out his line, but it unravelled and he lost the whole thing. He stomped back up to the store to get another one, while other workers slapped their thighs, cracking up in enjoyment. A basic, happy life on the beach.

The Algarve coast was my home for the day on my way to Sagres. I took a brief stop at the Three Brothers beach (Praia dos Três Irmãos) for a look to see if the sea stacks bore any resemblance to my brothers and me. One was small, one was skinny, and the other was fatter and better-looking. Pretty spot on for Kit, Patrick and me.

I skipped Faro and Lagos and started looking for potential wild camping spots for the night. A few vans were doing the same. They took up the more coastal cliff spots which were too blowy for my tent anyway. Plus, I'd likely be moved on by the authorities if found tenting it, hence turning off onto a back road through farmland. An old boy ploughed the field on his tractor as I turned the corner. The road then straightened with only enough room for a single vehicle on the smooth tarmac. I released the throttle, picturing the salt plains. A white horse galloped through a black field, emitting light like switching on a torch. Night-time had hit surprisingly fast, I thought, then took off my sunglasses. The field was green. There was more daytime left to play with. A large bird of prey rose out of the shrubbery and flew low across the field. We were neck and neck coming into the final stretch, completely parallel for a few seconds before it shot upwards and out of sight.

I found a windswept treeline inland. Right down on the south-west tip of Portugal. Out of curiosity, I followed the track further for a bit too long and hit soft sand. Just managing to hold on to the bike, using my feet on both sides, I stabilised and turned around to get back onto harder ground. Back wheel spinning, casting sand out behind, I made it through without toppling over. I rode the bike into a hedge in the treeline and found a gap just big enough for it, the tent and me (hunched over inside, but it made for good cover). No toilet paper disposed of here but I wasn't about to go digging. Jimmy resumed his usual hanging position from a branch. A lighthouse was close by, and the sweeping light caught my glance a few times as I raised a red glass to Tasha's birthday. I sat out front of the night's accommodation, contemplating the plan for the next day, and finished everything I could eat that didn't require cooking.

The next morning was an early one. Greeted by squeaking trees, then rain. In surfer-beach territory, I was keen to surf-watch from the safe distance of the shore. My ankle was not up to the task of surfing. The weather was a murky drizzle, increasing in volume. I didn't stick around for long, standing in the rain. A few people were out in the morning waves, many more chilling on the high cliff bank in front of their vans, weighing up if or when to dip their toes.

notes

- it is possible to swim to the Benagil Caves, but the current can be strong. Boards or kayaks are better. Be prepared to get wet

24
THE CASCADE
TO CASCAIS

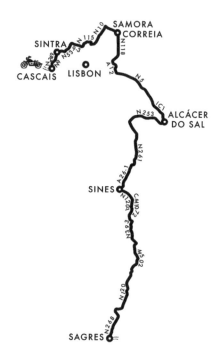

The only way to go from here was north. Due to the forecasted weather, I didn't "Mess Around". Ray Charles had been on my playlist that morning. The road just kept on going, prompting me to follow. No doubt I missed out on some beautiful spots and attractions, and I don't recall being in a rush, but ever since leaving Tarifa it felt like I was heading home.

After an hour that felt like three, I stopped for breakfast in a small café sat in a little bay with shallow waters, separated from the sea only by the road. Behind the café, a few rows of stacked houses had pokey windows and steep driveways. Handbrakes firmly on. A handful of van travellers sat cramped around an outside table under the shelter, chatting in English. Seeing out the winter in the region, working and surfing. I didn't catch much more of their conversation, being immersed in the ham-and-cheese-croissant-and-espresso dream combo, sat in my own exposed puddle. It had been an early and wet morning to kick-start the day, and it rained still. I didn't long for home, but I was thinking about it more often in the bad weather.

Due to the rain, the map on my phone started to make its own decisions. The water had got into the case and was acting as my finger. Putting pressure on the screen caused it to exit Maps, open something else, close that, open another app, and so on. I would stop, dry it, then five minutes later it would do the same. This induced lots of wrong turns as a result, followed by pauses to amend, slowing down the morning ride. Every cloud has a silver lining, though; I saw some smart Mercedes and a few remote spots on these unplanned detours.

Lunchtime. A beach café with surf rental by Sines was perfectly placed. A hip couple stood in the car park, sussing out the waves. Apparently a storm was on the horizon and "the swell would be tragic, dude". Inside, with a baguette and coffee, I planned the remainder of the day. I wasn't in the mood for enduring Lisbon on this trip, as having the hassle of my belongings strapped to the back without locks, and accommodation and traffic to deal with, was more than I felt I could manage. I drew a route over the top to Cascais on the coast above. The start of a well-reviewed coastal road continuing north. Maps reckoned it was around a four-hour-straight ride. On top of the three hours I'd already done. I felt good and thought I had it in me. Providing it was dry for the most part.

It rained for the rest of the day in intervals. Proper heavy downpours every half hour. The roads were great, though. Wide, long and changing scenery with interesting sections of houses, farms and businesses, then pastures. The cold and wetness of my gear soon surpassed the pleasure, causing me to stop at least three times for coffee, each time pouring more water out of my boots. The rain was so dense at one point that I couldn't see through the visor at all. I was relieved there was less traffic than the English M27 as the weather was worse. I wiped the visor with my forefinger then regripped the handlebar. Visibility was immediately halted as I was encased in water again. I left my hand there, forefinger imitating windscreen wipers. *This is ridiculous.* I had to stop. I turned off the highway to stand under a tree. This only stopped the flow for a few minutes before another break in the rain.

The saving grace of sun arrived in the fields before Lisbon as the city in the distance emerged, poking its head up and over a petrol station in a neighbouring district.

There was no newspaper, old or new, at Camping Orbitur Cascais to stuff my boots with. I questioned the need for an ironing board with no iron on my way to the showers. It had a useful facility block with outside plugs to charge my portable battery pack, although I had to leave it unattended overnight. There was a decent shop with everything needed for an early dinner and bed. Sagres to Camping Orbitur Cascais = 360 km (how many miles?) done in one day. Over half the length of Portugal's coastal road.

25
THE POIGNANT PONG
OF PENICHE

Another patchy morning meant there was no desire to leave until midday. The long ride the day before was the main contributor to the lazy start. The N247 for the most part was a restricted speed limit in a built-up area, yet in parts it did hold some saucy scenes. Extravagant restaurants sat on rock edges, surrounded by flickering sand. Golden specks swept across the roads as impressive black clouds gathered out to sea, heading my way, sparking worry.

As the road climbed around the hillside, different layers appeared with their skewed gardens. Villages had misleading turnings, and I missed directions more than once.

A common passing scene was of elderly men sat roadside on chairs, chatting and watching the world go by. On a village corner where the road touched the houses was a large set of garage double doors. A rounded fellow sat in view, flat cap over his face and arms dangling down by the side of his chair. I couldn't hear the snoring over the sound of the bike but I pictured it so.

I was conned into an incredibly tasty €23 lunch at an authentic Portuguese restaurant directly west from Torres Vedras, in a small place called São Pedro da Cadeira. This was the seafood dinner I had missed in France. A range of starters was brought out that I hadn't selected. I ate them all, without knowing you pay for what you have. I ate all ten unpeeled prawns, the bread, a type of cranberry sauce, garlic aioli, tinned pâté, mixed salad, chopped sausage, crackers, and the little battered things. I awaited my order of fish soup that I'd heard the area was famous for. It never came. Turns out I'd ordered the wrong dish. It was, however, a delectable grilled fresh fish with potatoes. No complaints whatsoever. And for the money it was reasonable; I just didn't expect I needed to eat that much.

notes

- I was given a pen on my departure. Ponto Final was the restaurant, in São Pedro da Cadeira. Extremely welcoming, with a restaurant or separate café option

The pong of Peniche. The potent fish pranced around my nasal cavities, playing havoc with the senses. A proper seaside fishing town with port 'n' all. Windy too. The town protrudes from the mapped line of the coast on a rocky peninsula. The ferry port and car park sat opposite a small maritime bar. *Will check that out later.* Giant stone anchors were stacked together to form a sea wall, marked with a few tags like "so-and-so woz 'ere". Senior men huddled together on a double bench, wrapped up warm in protection from the wind, looking like rockhopper penguins – large bushy eyebrows, pointy gelled hair and stubby beaks.

I followed the outskirts, past the ageing prison fort museum, out onto the north side. Here, there were no longer any walls; waves crashed straight over the edge of the rocks, seawater smashing against the windowpanes of buildings. The wind caught the bike and tried to throw me off to the left. Jimmy would hold on until the end, no doubt. In the commotion I managed to plant my stronger foot and catch the bike with a shuffle of hands. The wing mirror got a light scratch but that was all. I rode at a snail's pace thereafter, with a queue of cars behind that just had to wait.

Finding a campsite was hard and there were none in Peniche. A short ride away was Baleal, which had one. My phone was out of battery as the dodgy phone cable didn't work unless it was perfectly still, which was a rarity. I got a little lost down some sandy roads, surrounded by that potent farm smell of chicken shit. A power-line cable had broken off the pole and was swinging in the road. Possibly just passable but I turned back, avoiding the risk of shock.

The startled look from the camp owner when I asked for a tent pitch made me question if she knew something that I didn't. She said, "It's better to rent small units in this weather." I believed she was trying to upsell me.

After consulting with Jimmy, I stupidly held firm and only paid the small fee for camping. I sat in the reception café area for warmth and Wi-Fi for much of the evening. It was getting time to head home. I could feel it. I looked at ferries from Santander and Bilbao, estimating that I could get there in roughly a week at a comfortable pace. The downside of booking last minute. I was informed that as it's a quiet time of year, the ferries go in for their version of an MOT. As such, there was not a single available spot for the next couple of weeks. December was fast approaching. I booked the first available place, then pondered on the option of following the coast all the way round through Galicia or cutting inland. Truth be told, I was about ready for the comfort of my Uggs. I ordered a takeaway beer for the tent, thanked the owner for my free cheese pastry and went on to bed.

It's Saturday at 03.05 having just looked at my phone. It's like someone has an industrial fan on the highest setting, pointed at a fixed plastic bag. It was windy when I went to sleep, but fuck me, it's heavier now. I jump out. Fortunately, the rain isn't too heavy, and I can get pegs back in the ground with relative ease. Back in the tent, it feels like I'm an inch tall and inside that plastic bag. Water is pooling in the lowest corner. I soak it up with socks then take some of my bags to the large toilet block and leave them there. The wind is ferocious. I won't sleep. I put on my headphones and listen to classical music, wondering if the camping stint of the trip is over. I should have rented the small unit! I manage to get off to sleep.

A gorgeous morning followed, apart from the smell of rot that travelled in the wind from neighbouring farms. I couldn't help but laugh at the poorly placed location of this campsite. The sun shone in stark contrast to the night I'd endured. I sat outside reading *The Buddha of Brewer Street*, enjoying a generous 5 p.m. check-out time, while everything dried out on a self-erected bright-pink washing line. The owner gave warning of an incoming storm that had been forecast. "Was that not it last night?" I asked in dismay. It was not.

I headed back to Peniche to find a hostel where I could spend the weekend. It was time for a real roof and livelier atmosphere. At Baleal beach, part of the World Championship surf competition that year, I watched some decent surf and contemplated renting again, but my ankle still didn't feel up to it. Although it had stopped throbbing, it taunted me at the thought of boarding.

I checked into Aktion Hostel and was one of five guests plus a monkey in a 120-person-capacity hostel. I would recommend the place. Cheap enough at €12 a night, and loads of room for activities in this huge converted warehouse. Pleasant staff. Lager on tap.

The little bar I'd spotted earlier was as interesting as I thought it would be. Maritime trophies, photos and model ships decorated the only small bar room. A group of ten-odd lads drank bottled beers and watched football on the telly, whilst an elderly couple ran the show. Shortly after I sat down, they gathered around the small bar, throwing banter around in Portuguese. One man flamed a sausage on a purpose-built terracotta dish. He poured alcohol in the base and sparked it, casting sea-like flames as he turned the sausage on the bars above. A delicacy, I was told. A bit burnt, but spot on with bread and a laugh at the half-cut chef.

Peniche Fortress. A must-visit. Over-the-average merry, I wobbled around looking at the various images screened on projectors. I quickly sobered up. The large sixteenth-century prison sits at the mouth of the harbour and was used by the military up until 1897. Since then, it's been used in a variety of ways. Boer refugees from South Africa sheltered there in the early twentieth century, German and Austrian prisoners were held here during the First World War, and it's stood as a museum since 1984. The most striking history, however, and the main part of the museum, was Salazar's "Estado Novo" (new state) period spanning from 1934 to 1974, during which time communist supporters against the corporatist regime (close to fascism) were imprisoned here.

Upon entry, a blonde painted bridge walkway had been weathered by sea air. It rose above a small bay down to the left. Waves rallied through the arch into the bay, lashing the cliff walls. Bright green grass emerged out of every conceivable crevice on the crumbling stone above the rocky steps that led to the rubble beach. The prison cells were visible and family visitor rooms could be explored. Etched into the glass that separated the visitor and prisoner meeting area was: "Fale mais alto! Só pode falar da sua família." (Speak louder! You can only talk about your family.) It wasn't as brutal as the S-21 prison in Cambodia, but still, a dark history where prisoners were kept in poor conditions.

On the floor of a cramped isolation cell, which I thought was a great story, a plaque read:

Escape of António Dias Lourenço

The escape of António Dias Lourenço from the "Segredo", the isolation cell of the Round Fort, took place on 17 December 1954.

He purposely forced punishment so as to be kept in the "Segredo". For days, and with the help of a knife, he removed the timber from the cell door and made himself a rope out of a shredded blanket, which he used to jump to the sea.

Once he reached the shore, next to the fish auction sale, Dias Lourenço was aided by a fisherman who carried him covertly in a fish van to Bombarral. He found help from there.

Back at the hostel a few more guests had checked in by the time I returned. We got on well as we cooked our own dinners and sat around outside sharing stories, weighing up whether to head to Baleal beach nightclub. Deciding against it, we partook in an international cigarette instead. Chile, Italy, Germany, Poland, Portugal, USA and England were all present at the table of democracy. We could have fixed the world that night if given the chance, but we opted for table tennis and beers instead.

All day Sunday was wet. I finished *The Buddha of Brewer Street* and rated it highly.

Next stop with a break in the weather was Nazaré to the north – home of the waves and several Guinness World Records.

26
WHAT WAVES?

There were no waves to speak of as I sat with coffee overlooking a concrete pier and the famous lighthouse of Nazaré. *Typical. The one day I'm here.* At least the ride up was decent. Not right on the sea edge but high on a ridge, with rolling greenery to the right, shaded in by dotted settlements and bunches of trees, and on the left, the partially natural coastline and vast ocean. The next land mass being the USA.

Disappointed not to see these record breaking waves, I mounted the Shadow and followed the road up through the town, on a steep hill past the market, heading seaward. Cobbled streets led onto a loose stone car park and a sizeable scaffolding arch with a surfing advertisement spread across the width. People walked up and down through it. Mostly down. An "Authorised Vehicles Only" sign hugged a pole as I rode past.

The famous lighthouse I'd seen earlier wasn't the right one. At the bottom of the hill stood the one I then recognised from pictures and surfing videos. A large billboard with the same surfer sign was surrounded by a crowd of wave watchers. There were waves! If they were still classed as such at that size. Four jet skis out to sea towed surfers on sets of humongous waves in a competition – Nazaré Tow Surfing Challenge – waiting their turn for the right one to come along. A powerful surge, one of the most incredible natural forces, caused by the canyon below; averaging between twelve and eighteen metres high but reaching twenty-plus, some sources claim. Not all year round as it was very much sea-and-swell dependent; best between October and March, I was informed. They were colossal. I was gobsmacked.

I took the Atlântica road which was more coastal than the main route. Free of traffic and with space to roam with views of dunes. *I should have filled up in Nazaré.* Here was a straight road as far as you could see, with mounds up and down like a pump track. Either side of the road were remains of burnt trees, and younger, furry bushes appeared to be levitating, tickling the sand.

Small, desolate villages followed, and then random piles of logs, ten metres long and stacked neatly like Jenga rather than Pick-Up Sticks. After riding long into my reserve tank, I found a rural station for fuel and pulled up to the pump.

Fuck! I've lost my keys!

My bike keys were in the ignition – riding without them would have been questionable – but my set for the brake lock, chain lock, box panniers and metal security netting around my luggage. I hit a peculiar feeling of panic. I didn't recall when I had them last. I had no choice but to laugh it off. I'd survive with spares for all except one: the padlock that secured the metal netting which housed my tent, sleeping bag and clothes. I could buy a new padlock somewhere easily enough but getting the old one off would be problematic with my penknife or spanner. I'd be hacking for days! The station had a garage next door which might have helped, but then lay the issue of keeping it secure as there were no padlocks for sale in the shop. I opted to ride on in the hope that the destination would have lower-hanging fruit.

After I'd arrived in Aveiro, the daylight faded fast, almost majestically together with my phone at an espresso stop. The charging cable was no more, the connection damaged. I accepted I'd be riding around the maze of busy one-way streets, asking in places that had the option to park outside, counting the stars then moving on if it had too many. With no granted access to the tent, camping was out of the question. I bit the stingy bullet and paid for a hostel in a modest four-bedroom establishment off the main streets, with on-road motorbike parking. It rained all night and I thanked my lucky stars I forked out. I unfastened Jimmy and everything else extractable, leaving the remains up for grabs. I hoped someone would break the padlock, realise there was nothing of value, then leave it open for me in the morning.

With a freshly purchased phone charger, I endured a sour London Pride pint at a craft beer pub, still in motorbike gear. Everyone was wearing coats, their breath visible. There was four people in the bar, and the barman refused to close the door when it was eight degrees outside. Not the homely, warm, English-bar vibe they were aiming for.

After pizza at a café blaring out "Down Under", I was ready for bed. Outside was a canal with parked gondola-like boats that persuaded a pause and appreciation, with a colourful array of buildings stacked either side like Hotwells in Bristol.

Showered, changed and lying in bed, I discovered my new cable and adaptor were missing. I searched the room and bag with no luck. *The sour-pint pub!* I'd taken it there earlier.

It was still open, and I was pleased to see that the door was now closed when I got there to retrieve them. I'd have stayed for a couple more if they'd closed the door earlier!

Fully charged the following morning, I was met by the modern challenge of the hostel kitchen. Ceramic hobs in general are a bloody pain. I persevered by putting my percolator into a purpose-built pan with boiling water to brew my morning coffee.

My bike and luggage parked on the road were untouched and intact. No shops that I could find sold or lent bolt cutters. In an industrial estate I rode into a do-it-yourself vehicle wash station to use the hose before locating a garage. As I was there, I asked the weary attendant if he spoke English or Spanish, to which he replied, "Poco" – a little. He agreed to help but gave me a funny look, presumably wondering if I'd stolen the bike complete with a grubby monkey. Showing the rest of my keys, I won him over, then a moment later he came out with an angle grinder, dragging the cord behind him. Without time for me to move any luggage, he set to work, and I winced at the thought of him striking the bike or setting Jimmy alight. He cut the power, and with a smile he presented me with the penetrated padlock.

On leaving Aveiro, while at a cross junction and sharing a smiling wave with the truck driver above me, I made the decision to head inland, throwing the throttle as soon as green graced us, skipping Porto, Northern Portugal, and the Galicia region in Spain. I headed for León.

I reached the N222, which would be the road for the next hundred kilometres as I followed the Douro River through the valley.

The gardens glowed in dark shades of autumnal red, green and orange as I left Canedo for Lomba. At a communal village washbasin, shaped like a four-poster bed, two hunched ladies washed and scrubbed clothes, just before the path descended to a beach park fitted with BBQs, water taps, toilets … the works. I would have stopped there for the night if there hadn't been a surplus of roads to tackle and the daily issue of dinner before nightfall, which was getting earlier with each passing day.

"Slalom" was the concluding word. Although the N222 had some variety, I pulled off on some CM roads for tighter turns and struggled to keep up with a small red Corsa as it hurtled downhill before meeting an oncoming bus in the middle of the road and swerving at the last possible moment. Thanks to my lack of cornering ability, and the IAM course two-second following rule ("Only a fool breaks the two-second rule"), I was far enough behind to skip into safety.

As it grew darker, I withdrew my excitement for slaloming and began looking for a tent spot. A large park on a river had potential, again with all the necessary leisure facilities. Large "No Camping" signs were scattered around. Not so much of an issue in the November cold, I considered, as I wandered the paths. The church I'd passed was in hymn, which echoed out across the valley in hypnotic, almost seismic, vibrations. In stark contrast it was soon interrupted by what sounded like an ice cream van blaring its yearning tune. Firstly, it was not the weather for ice cream, and secondly, it was not an ice cream van.

The short-wheelbase truck roamed the empty roads. Its curtain sides opened to the back, revealing large speakers tied down inside throwing jolly Christmas-like music out into the valley.

notes
- this occurred on 19 November. I have found no reason or significance as to the purpose of the music truck. Much to my disappointment

Adhering to the park signs, I rode up the next hill, over, then down to the next possible place to park. In contrast to the usual method of stopping, I switched off the engine and coasted through a set of tightly packed houses, pulling off the main road. I glided down their steep drive before reaching a gravel opening. There was a long, thin grassy area on the other side of the car park. It had a small wooden walkway bridge further up, inaccessible to bikes. A docking area lay alone in the river, no boats for company. High walls separated this area from solid but crumbling buildings, grand gardens, and vegetable patches on higher ground. Under a tree I set up camp, with the bike parked on the gravel thirty metres away. I shuttled back and forth with my gear, popping Jimmy where he's most comfortable, in the branches above. I moved the large green wheelie bin in front of the bike to shield it from view, then covered the chrome with a tarp to hinder the revealing shine.

In utter tranquillity I sat on my throne, the river at my feet. The green and orange of the valley hillside opposite swirled around white pimpled farmhouse buildings. Low layers of cloud shifted briskly over peaks, and ripples in the water were seen, not heard. The farm's fruit fields waved in lines like forehead wrinkles.

The silence was cracked by the rumble of a train running alongside the river on the opposite side to me. Off it chugged. The ripples in the water became noisy splashes as fish came up for a glance. Dogs started barking, and that was it for the still night. Yet it was the green flashing light on a buoy that drove me to bed, not the cold or the dogs, and I warmed up by rubbing Tabasco in my eye, which streamed into my makeshift pillow.

27
SMUGGLERS' WAY

A misty morning. A commuting plump of ducks sliced the icing that was lathered on thick atop the river. My breath was visible throughout the morning's procedures. Overnight, a ferocious-looking spider had taken shelter in my helmet, reappearing only as I put it on and quickly retracted my head. *I'm fine with*

spiders. I'm fine with spiders. I'm fine with spiders ... Without leaving a trace I left to tackle the overcast day.

Back on the N222 I pulled in at the Régua Dam Lock. While waiting for a boat, I looked back from the direction I came. Two bridges crossed the river before veering off in different directions on the other side. One was obviously newer in its design: a curved motorway flyer that enhanced the beauty of the natural surroundings instead of imposing on it. No boat used the lock system, which was a shame.

The low-lying cloud was impossible to escape. I stopped a few times in admiration. Small patches congregated below the hilltop, like bunched-up sheep huddling for warmth.

As I was in a renowned port-and-wine region, I considered a tasting session. Having to ride afterwards would have been too tormenting, though, so I stopped in Pinhão for coffee and pastry instead where the N222 left the riverside.

Eight dogs cruised down the cobbled streets like they owned the place. Everyone stopped to look but they didn't glance back. They just strolled on past like *Scooby Doo* met *West Side Story*.

I took the wrong road at Pinhão which ascended onto the IC5. Bridged between the tops of rolling hills, it was a motorway that climbed higher the closer I got to Spain. It was adequately named; from an icy cold rating of one to five it was a solid five, and the gradual incline ceased all feeling in my fingers and toes. Comfort was required. I pulled off at the next exit in search of civilisation and a hot meal.

A large truck-stop restaurant with two dirt track entrances either side of a forlorn seesaw and swing set was a good enough reason to stop. It must have just gone midday as I climbed the steps and entered the packed restaurant. The round tables were full except for a couple by the door. I felt piercing eyes on me as they put down their lunchtime drinks for a moment before returning to their food, conversation or TV, as I stood close to shivering in the doorway, dripping over their floor. The extremely friendly staff at Restaurante O Careca spoke no English, but we conversed enough in basic Spanish to understand one another. I understood "carne" and "patatas" so ordered that. Meat and potatoes, which came with a whole basket of bread. Typical of the area and darn good.

I pulled the map out after eating, and ordered a bucket of coffee. On the waiter's return, I asked where we were, gesturing to the open map on the table in front of me.

"Carrazeda de Ansiães," he responded then repeated, with clear enough pronunciation for me to appreciate.

It was a working town that I expected would brighten up in the summer, and I guessed it offered glorious walking routes from the scenery I'd passed. This was a grey November day. It appeared to long for the summer months. Refuelled and of a sounder mind, I decided on our route, opting for the N214 rather than submitting ourselves to the death road they call the IC5. It was about an extra hour's riding, but even in those conditions I couldn't face getting back on that dreaded motorway. The N214 was a splendid road, with short straights, curving dips and a quality surface that weaved through one-shop villages and their one bar – usually with people spilling out the front. The rains had held off for a while, hence the roads were drier than they had been for days. Still bitterly cold at 1°C, I headed for Bracança, close to the Spanish border in the north-east of Portugal.

The rains came on the N206. Another stunning road that descended down through a valley in the mist. Gloves wet, hands wetter, after a ninety-minute ride since lunch I pulled in at a sporadically used bus stop surrounded by gallant forest. I lit the gas stove and my hands cupped it close to touching as I'd lost all feeling. Without realising, I sat on the sodden bus bench and picked up the green moss with my cheeks. I didn't even get to make a cuppa, as I couldn't prize open the pot. I partially warmed up before riding on, leaving a perfect arse print waiting for the bus.

A fast-food restaurant was again useful for Wi-Fi. I sat in a familiar puddle with a warming green tea and found a hostel online. On arrival the reception wasn't open until 5 p.m. and I was two hours early. I was done. A soggy, wrinkle-stricken, wormlike mess of a man. After using the toilets to moisturise my itchy skin, I waited in the lobby warmth to thaw and fell asleep on their sofa. Not a bad price at €13 for the night in a shared four-bed dorm at HI Hostel. My only roommate arrived after I'd gone to sleep. At around 5 a.m. their phone went off, and yet it did not wake them. I booted their bed and still they would not wake. I got up to find the ringing phone. I stood over the bed without realising I was being creepy. I urged them to turn it off. They woke.

They proceeded to avoid me the following morning, which I tried to resolve. A natural talent of mine is to fall back asleep instantly, so I didn't mind.

After coffee, I pottered about Bracança for an hour on the bike. Overlooking the city was an extraordinary citadel enclosed by great walls. Dating back to the twelfth century, yet in near pristine condition, the citadel had an interesting trade history and was set in beautiful, remote surroundings. An espresso and cigarette stop later and I was back on the open road, sun shining with a fresh chill.

There are a few options to cross the border when heading for León, and I opted for the small N218-3 road before turning right onto the N308, where a green garden gate led to a miniature white building standing at around six feet – a shrine – enclosed by a white wall a foot high. The road sign declared "Varge" and "Río de Onor". Varge came first, a quiet village. As I turned into the square, a man and his working horse walked across the cobbled centre. I parked up and was caught by surprise as I came face-to-face with a red-faced demon holding a long club in both hands, dressed in robes of all colours. It became apparent that he was there to greet visitors; in this case, Jimmy and me. *I must get a photo of this.* No reference was made to its symbolic meaning. I wandered around and pictured village scenes, made a note to investigate further and moved on, leaving via a single bridge crossing the river, in view of the three-storey stone buildings and their wooden balconies.

notes

- the Careto tradition is a prehistoric Celtic ritual linked to the winter solstice. Single young men dressed as demons parade the village, creating chaos and taking gifts – "robbing" people – before being united with the single young women over dinner and dancing

Between the two villages were 14.5 km of racetrack roads through the green bushland of the natural park of Montesinho. Quite possibly more lovely than the Douro Valley due to its remoteness. Much colder, too, as higher up, with snow-capped mountains in the background that topped it off. I increased the speed as I rode past two men in their country wear cradling shotguns.

A handful of buildings hadn't lasted the previous winter and were left crumbled, roofs caved in. Those that remained stood close by, urging their structures not to be next as the colder months approached. A shit dog shot out of the rubble. It followed me through streets barely wide enough for a car, yapping its heart out until I left its territory.

Río de Onor, part Portugal, part Spain, was a picturesque village split by a river, with well-tended vegetable patches and flourishing scarecrows, seemingly unphased with the wider world.

At the other end of the village was the blue sign announcing Spain. *We meet again.* It felt like a smugglers' route on the single roads through woodland and over hills. I was riding cautiously due to black ice, getting closer to the snowy peaks. A 4x4, complete with trailer, came hurtling round the corner, forcing a manoeuvre onto a grass verge. "Phew!" I gasped as I pulled back onto the road. I veered off again as a party of four synchronised dogs in a diamond formation were following in hot pursuit, a border collie leading the way.

Once through Puebla de Sanabria, one of the oldest settlements in the Zamora region of Spain, I stopped for coffee in a large hotel by a service station and paid the price for it: €10 for espresso and a pastry. A bloody rip-off! But they were banging.

The cold had really been getting to me. No handguards, no grip warmers; only my summer gloves, jeans and jacket. My own terrible choices, so no sympathy expected. With each coffee stop I found warmth, caffeine-infused energy, optimism and eagerness for the next stint. Jimmy was still yet to complain.

28
LEANING IN LEÓN

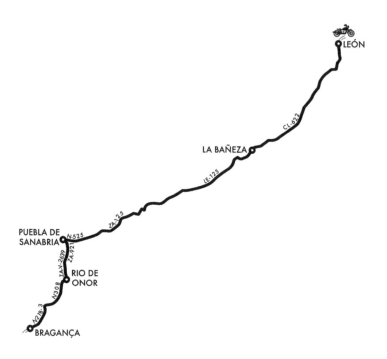

León lay littered with churches and cathedrals, dating back to the tenth and thirteenth centuries, with an array of towers and tombs. The most notable was the Catedral de Santa María and its vast Gothic architecture, along with Convento de San Marcos, considered the most important renaissance building in the country and now a grand hotel.

I made little progress through the one-way streets, circling round trying to follow signs. At the third hostel, I paid for a cheap bed in a mixed dormitory of more than twenty-five beds, Check In León. Clean, communal and parking outside. The unavoidable snoring that came later was expected and prepared for (cue essential earplugs). An abundance of supposedly better hostels was scattered around the centre but with no vehicle access or parking, so this did just grand.

Refreshed, warm and cleaner, I wandered in the general guessed direction of a bar. I threw myself into a local place, sat down, ordered a drink, and in part interacted with the developing scenes as they circled around me. Typical nightfall new-place activity when travelling alone. I could not have foreseen the scene that unfolded next.

The sound of traffic persists through the cold air, both sensations piercing my jacket hood to reach my red ears. I'm not in the quiet warmth of Almería any more, that's for sure, but I can taste the rosy-red wine on my lips just the same. The street is dark and parked cars face both ways. I keep walking. I'll stop in the first bar I find.

Okay, not this one. The place looks empty. I'll put that down to the après-ski music blaring through the open, rattling door. Here's another. Large windows, frosted over for privacy but with sounds of chatter pouring out. The Mahou logo is engraved in each one. The smell of cigar smoke is rife around the porch area where the public pavement is covered with cigarette butts and two men smoke their cigars. Could be a member's bar. Let's try it. I reach the front door after stepping through hot coals.

Tables of cards and vocal Spaniards are my first sight. A mass of coats hang on a rack backed up against the opposite wall. The remains of old walls that have been knocked through still stand, splitting the canary yellow walls; it's now open plan, separated by a step. If I tilt my head and squint a little, the rack looks like a person swinging from the rail. I hang my coat and head to the bar, casting a gaze over a winning hand. Poker, I think, but there's no money or chips on the table. The floor has had a good night. Not nightclub-dance-floor sticky, but some real resistance for sure. Small bits of rubbish are swept up against the bar, yet to be picked up. One customer throws their napkin onto the floor. Seems to be the done thing.

The barman, the youngest person in there apart from me, pours my red wine and pulls out a plate of bread, sliced cooked meat and some hard cheese onto the bar. I take a spare pew and observe the games of cards taking place. There's a rotation of people at the bar as men stop for a swift lager and tapas then leave. A woman runs back and forth between groups of people. She grins her red wine teeth. Amusing conversations must be taking place.

"Where are you from?" The barman asks as he pours my second glass.

"Inglaterra," I reply.

Brief broken conversation and huge grins follow as I imitate a motorbike. With a nod of understanding, he serves another customer and I'm left to my refilled small plate.

Sipping my freshly poured third glass, in my right peripheral I see an elderly chap, shorter and stockier than I am, wearing a knitted grey jumper and sat on an identical stool to myself, maybe two metres away. He's bald, with a cross-shaped plaster on top of his head, two of those water-resistant ones – actually, one on top of the other – and hasn't been there long; his small lager is almost full, still frothy three-quarters of the way up the glass.

He inspects the bar counter with finite precision. His face is but an inch from the surface. Leaning over at almost forty-five degrees, his head passes the edge of the bar, and I'm reacting. He's out cold and falling fast. I drop my wine and it spills across the bar, causing a ruckus. It feels like time has slowed but I still can't act fast enough. No second thought for the wine, I manage to grasp under his fallen limp arm, right under his pit, freeing my right hand to cradle his head. I can't catch him completely, he's too heavy, so I fall with him. There's a silver footrest pole at the base of the bar which my elbow connects with – it would have been his head.

I make a sound from my mouth to alert others, but I can't make out what sound it is as I'm on the floor with him in my arms and he's still unconscious. He needs to go in the recovery position as he's sprawled out. I'm on my knees now, next to him on the floor filth. But I'm pulled back in shouts of words I don't understand, by people who must know him and don't know me. I stand and watch them take over.

Now the scene is surrounded by almost everyone in the bar. Two men try to lift him up. He's still unconscious. DON'T DO THAT! Someone else shouts not to pick him up as I repeat the same message in mumbling agreement, again unsure what sounds I've made. One of the men holding his limp left arm lets go and it flays back onto the ground.

Through a gap between shoulders in front of me, I push through and down onto my knees once again. Seven-year-expired lifeguard training here we go. I roll him over on his side and into the recovery position, ignoring everyone else around me. Just like that he comes round. Dark eyes stare straight ahead, with no initial movement, meaning or awareness. He then tries to get up, and we support his weight.

I step back at this point and ask for a glass of water: "Agua! Agua! Por favor." The dribble from his mouth is wiped away. I can tell by the helpers' intonation they're asking him questions but I don't know what. He didn't seem to recall anything. He's now sat up on the floor. Someone grabs a bar stool. Don't be daft, I mutter, not knowing the translation. Another gets a proper chair and he's lifted onto it and given a glass of water.

Chattering starts to happen, and just like that everyone turns around and carries on their card game as the ambulance is en route. The man is accompanied by another, who inspects the plaster and assumes it's happened to him before.

"Que pasó?" is asked in my direction by a fellow bar stander. I try to tell him what happened.

The bartender catches the conversation and laughs as I ask if he speaks English: "Hablas Inglés?"

I'm the only English speaker there, so no witness questions are asked.

Upon returning to the bar, once everything had settled down and I had caught my breath, my wine glass was full.

The poorly man was shipped out by the paramedics after their prompt arrival.

notes

- a famous city for architecture and a popular stop for Camino de Santiago walkers, some of whom I met at the hostel

29
SKY-TO-SEA HIGHWAY

As I left León it was bitter and full of puddles. No disrespect to the city, as from the little I saw it appeared to have a lot going for it, but I wasn't in a position to hang around. Another time maybe. It was about 140 km to Gijón on the north coast, a three-hour ride avoiding motorway tolls, and due to the conditions, likely longer. I started by cruising well below the speed limit. Thick forest was consistent either side while the rains quickly changed to snow as I climbed the N-630. To start, it was just your average road with long, straight restricted sections and traffic lights aplenty. I was overtaken frequently by large four-wheel drives lapping up the conditions. There would have been more room to ride on a dry day. The snow piled high in the forests further up and flowed across the road in slippery slush.

At Casa Senén, a restaurant in Vega de Gordón, one of the many small settlements nestled in the mountainside that hug the N-630, I made a mess in the corner. Soaked. Drenched. Doused. Lathered. Almost immersed in water. I propped up the radiator, gently caressing it as I drank my bucket of coffee, and then another, avoiding Jimmy's glare as he tended to the bike outside in the falling snow. More and more snow the higher I climbed. As you'd guess.

Approaching the road's peak of 1,300 metres, the white carpet grew thicker still as the temperature dropped. There was just enough traffic to stop it settling on the roads, but they were slushy still. Before the peak, visibility was not great. I felt enclosed and could sense the surroundings were mammoth in size, but I couldn't see the mountains that covered me.

At the peak, the sky opened. It stopped snowing. The sky turned cerulean blue with scattered clouds, and the peaks portrayed a reminder of homecoming. I couldn't process if that was a positive feeling or not. A rainbow cast out of the mountainside resided across the sky. I stopped and removed my glove, baring my hand to the frosty air to pull out my phone and get a picture.

I've done it. It was all downhill from here.

And it was for the rest of the day. I toppled over the edge of the steep downhill road, crawling at this point, pulling in to allow cars to pass by. Melting snow followed the spinal curvature of the hillside. The feeling in my hands and feet started to painfully return as I descended deeper into the valley, using my padded grips as stress toys, each squeeze like wearing gloves filled with pins.

notes

- many birds of prey, presumably eagles, soared overhead, which was just sensational
- in this area there are some superb roads that I was recommended to explore; however, conditions prevented finding them

On a stretch of motorway I had the chance to dry out my jeans. My legs spread wide and my crotch rose high above the tank. The whiff of wet dog channelled up to my helmet.

In a standard prepay fuel-station-slash-workers-bar, customers sat smoking in a covered area not ten metres from the pumps. Then the rains came again and there was no waiting it out.

Heading east from Gijón, following the coast where possible, a number of beaches received possible sleeping-spot enquiries. The weather looked calm at this point and I deemed it manageable for the night. Three campsites were closed, so I was on the wild hunt. I scrambled on foot down to a few tracks to see if they were possible to ride down, sweating profusely when returning to the bike. The most exercise I'd done on the trip! I'd already stocked up on cheese, rice, beans and wine for dinner.

A coastal stone track headed off into bushland and had three drop sections separated by flatter but still rocky ground. This led down to the coast. I skidded down the first drop, my feet either side. I then opted for jogging the next two as it was rough and risky, but I'd been looking for hours and was keen to take the chance. The Shadow lapped it up again – the extra height off the ground from the tyres certainly helped. *What a machine!* I flipped up its side stand, leaning it uphill. A walker's gate led to a cliff above the beach that had a path down. As scenic as any of the trip. The contrast between León in the morning and this point was drastic. I sat on the cliff edge and poured a glass. The wine was the worst drop of the trip, but staring north in the direction of home I thought how lucky I was , sitting in jeans and a jumper at 6.20 p.m., sundown but not yet dark. The ocean charged in and birds were still noisily going about their business. *This wine is really bad.* In the time my mug had been sitting on the grass, a slug had reached the top, indicating that I must have been nursing it. A slimy shock as I slurped unaware, my lips landing a sloppy slurp of slug. I was not so merry at that point. I had just a few nights to go before the ferry home from Santander.

30
WE BID YOU FAREWELL

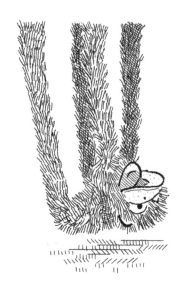

Final night in the tent timeline.

10.00 p.m. – Tucked away for the night after dinner, wine and a sing-song. *Weather report: a little windy but dry.*

1.00 a.m. – The fashioned porch-extension pegs came out. I woke up, ventured out and took it down. *Weather report: windy with light rain.*

3.50 a.m. – Tent collapsed. Thought it was the wind pushing the tent down when I first awoke. Lying on my back, arms stretched upwards, I held the poles at ten and two o'clock, wrestling with the wind. Tried to locate the break on the main pole whilst staying in bed, but it wasn't possible. Outside, I wedged the remaining length of pole into the ground and reinserted the rear pegs. The porch extension was repegged in and tied to the Shadow. Stable, albeit smaller than before. *Weather report: strong winds and heavy rain.*

4.20 a.m. – Main pole broke. Tent collapsed again. Tied guide ropes to the Shadow. The front of the tent was solely held up by the Shadow. Sat under the porch extension in wet clothes on a wetter chair. Shivering. Waited for another pole break. Thought about trying to get up the slope later that morning. Inside the tent, the bed was partially dry, plus some clothes in the dry bag. *Weather report: strong winds and heavy rain.*

4.40 a.m. – Tent bodged but stable. Checked the weather report: 40–45 kt winds. Pegs popped out at the back again. Hammered them back into a puddle, causing mud to the eye from splashback. Returned to my wet seat. *Weather report: fucking windy and persistent rain.*

5.00 a.m. – Tent bodged but stable. Took off shoes, socks, trousers and underwear, which were all wet through. Put on dry knickers. Got into bed. Coat still on. No sleep. *Weather report: constant bombardment.*

5.45 a.m. – Side pegs came out. Bursting for a piss with all the rainfall. Frustratingly, it was a long one standing in the rain, likely emptying all over my feet. Checked the official weather report: sunrise at 8.23 a.m. I was going to make it. Finished off the remainder of the red wine and tried rolling cigarettes. *Weather report: strong winds and heavy rain.*

6.15 a.m. – Bodged structure still standing! Air mattress now floating on water. Still in bed and managed some sleep. *Weather report: sleeping.*

8.20 a.m. – Woke. Sunrise. *Weather report: light wind and rain.*

31
ROSA

RIBADESELLA
AS-379
LLANES
N-634
SAN VICENTE
DE LA BARQUERA
CA-2.3
CA-131
N-611
SANTANDER

Digesting two pots of coffee, loud music and a soggy choccy croissant, I contemplated the next steps. First things first: I mortifyingly disassembled the torn, broken, dishevelled yet heroic tent. Some tosser left it standing in the field after Glastonbury Festival finished, for someone else to pick up their mess. Although I put this one to good use, there were hundreds more left to landfill. This one wasn't one of those one-use festival tents that are marketed by major retailers, which sparks the idea that people should leave them behind.

Exerting pent-up energy from being overtired and cramped in that porch most of the night, I ran up and down the grassy cliff area using the outer sheet as a kite. Every wet item hung off the handlebars, exhaust, forks, brakes and seats, trying to dry. Including Jimmy.

As I moseyed back to the pitch, it started to hail. I ran. Through the muddied gate I slid, flapping for balance. I launched the tent in the air, holding the end like shaking out a duvet, gently bringing it down over myself, the Shadow and my hanging clothes. Peering out the bottom I caught sight of two pairs of boots and four furry legs. A couple walked by with their pooch. I lifted the tent that caved around all my belongings. We looked at each other in dismay. I laughed. I had to. They joined in, then called something out in English that I couldn't hear over all the crying. I laughed and replied, as you do. *It is what it is.*

I was sad to say goodbye to my tent, but at least it was towards the end of the trip. I booked a hotel in Ribadesella, with the earliest check-in I could find: 3 p.m. My worry about the state of the off-road track was resolved as the Shadow lapped it up for breakfast, again with my feet either side like stabilisers.

The bedroom was a drying operation. My washing line was an array of bunting, tied from curtain rail to door to rail to bathroom to coat hanger to rail. The hotel specified that it had heating available; not that they put it on. I went downstairs barefoot in shorts and vest to request they turn it on. "Put some bleedin' clothes on," I heard them think.

"This is all I have that is dry!" I tried to say.

It switched off again after twenty minutes, so I disembarked for a two-hour round trip to the laundrette in my shorts.

A bar called El Farin opened its doors a moment before I entered. It was opposite my hotel and I was the first one in. I was soon joined by the hotel owner and a long-in-the-tooth local donning flat cap and wax jacket, drinking local cider (sidra, produced all over Asturias in Spain). A younger man in flash jeans arrived and bought a round for the whole bar, asserting his authority. *You crack on mate. Thanks!* Then soon afterwards, succulent battered calamari and fresh mussels were brought out and placed on the bar.

I was captivated by the bar owner's talent of pouring a bottle of sidra from a great height over the sink. Arms elongated, apart as far as they could muster. Cloudy sidra glugged out of the towering bottle held high above their head, then landed perfectly like a gymnast's dismount in the wide-berth glass that they held in the sink. I'd witnessed the process of oxygenating the sidra to enjoy the full flavour of the drink. *I've since tried this at home and would advise practising with water. Outside. Or at your friend's house.*

The old boy shot the couple of gulps back in one. Sat by him at the bar, I observed him and smiled in amusement at the process. He chortled and continued to drink this way all night, laughing after every pour, leaving the cork to roost on top of the bottle to signify it was still in use. I made a couple of roll-ups for us and we continued laughing outside. About what exactly, I'm a bit hazy on the details.

Tired, tipsy and full of fish, I toddled back across the street to my duvet and bed, with a wrapped bottle of sidra to take home.

The next day I took the long road to Santander. The ferry was a few days away. Boots, Jimmy, blanket and my boots were uncomfortably saturated, but I had to move on and check out on time. I rode on the AS-379, then enjoyed a beautiful ride on smaller roads that looped closer to the coast.

Revitalised after an espresso and Spanish tortilla, I had a swift walk around Llanes, a picturesque harbour town. The brightly coloured cubic wave breakers were a sight to behold, each painted in a unique design. The large stone blocks were placed to create a breakwater. This major work of art was truly intriguing.

I came out onto the N-634 and followed this for the most part. White-topped mountains emerged with wavy coastal roads. At San Vicente de la Barquera I had to pull in to catch my breath from the view, like reaching a level of unfamiliar altitude. Water besieged a grand church which came into view around a fast bend. Pure postcard material. Bridges sprung out from the central town like antlers, hectic with lone fishermen and their rods. Then I climbed up again through green hills, opting for the quieter CA-236.

At Oyambre beach, I stopped to watch the surf with a beer and espresso. Being a Sunday, the place was busy with locals. It had a great vibe with open beach views. Paul McCartney rocked up in his old Jag. It wasn't him, but I had to take my sunnies off to check.

The closer to Santander, the busier it got. Rolling green was still the backdrop, but buildings and farmland in the forefront became frequent. A line of trees on a hillside hugged the spine like the mohawk on a ridgeback – the last of the natural scenery before I joined a mix of urban roads into the centre.

I found Hostel de las Facultades with ease which made a nice change. I had booked two nights, paying extra for a shared room of four rather than twelve. I slept alone, which was well needed at the end of the trip. No alcohol was allowed in the hostel, which is fair enough, but apart from that it was a pretty decent place.

There was time to visit the Peninsula de la Magdalena, a coastal park that beckoned for walking and exploring. It would be busy in the summer months for sure, and I could picture families on picnic blankets and games of football on the luscious green lawns. On a sunny November midweek day, it was empty, perfect for roaming the gardens and admiring the coastal views.

As if you thought I'd done enough riding, I cruised around the outskirts of Santander luggage-free, turning nosily and noisily down small streets, soaking up the last of everything I could. I had been ready to go home for the past few weeks, but as the final day arrived, I wanted to carry on. *What was I going back to?*

I've got no job, so no money coming in. I've got no inspiring plan about what to do next. The next stage kept looping around my brain.

At almost midnight, my brother rang. In slumber, with the ferry early the next morning, I didn't sleep much after he gave me the news. Rudy had a little sister, and I had a niece, Rosa.

A magical moment to head home. I was absolutely buzzing. This is what I was going back for.

The daunting prospect of stepping back into the contrived environment they call the office was no more, and actually, the anticipation that I did not know what job was to come was as exhilarating as the open road and rush of wind. It had certainly been a merry ride round Iberia by bike.

The culminating image was of Spain from the ferry. A long stretch of land, propped up by the lapping bay, with a sombrero of shallow cloud that covered Santander and the mountains behind. One of the passengers only just caught the barrier as they were thrown forward onto the deck below. *I forgot about the foot passengers!*

The final stretch on British soil was as wet as the outward journey. Yet I stood smiling at the fuel station, filling up having not yet paid, optimistic about the next chapter.

Answer to the question in the introduction:

500 km ÷ 2 = 250
500 km ÷ 10 = 50 +

------

300 miles (roughly – exact answer is 310.69)

EPILOGUE

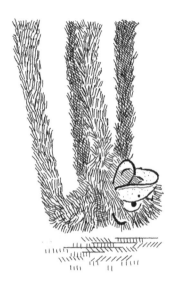

Heading home without knowing what my plan was, I knew I was privileged enough to have a supportive family who could roof my head for the time being. I am lucky to be able to have done this, to pack in my job and not have commitments or bills to pay unless I choose to. I can go on this trip, which so many don't have access to. If I fail in my next endeavours, I will have the support of my family to help me. It makes the risk easier to take, and for this I am eternally grateful. We were not a particularly well-off family, but we always had enough by the time I came around. Growing up, I would inherit my older brother Kit's hand-me-down clothes, which he got from our cousins. I would put holes in everything from any number of the outdoor activities I pursued, so my little brother, Patrick, never got the old garments. The youngest are always the most spoilt anyway.

I had a massive head start. I was born white, not in poverty or wartime, and I can travel and visit other communities and cultures. I hope to use it to contribute to making the world a better place, in any way I know how, to improve the quality of our natural environment, which we should all be fighting tooth and nail to protect. Not just using my privilege to benefit me, my image, my bank account and the shareholders.

At some point after returning home, I read *Bonjour! Is this Italy?* and thought, *I could do that.* I was an English Language and Literature A Level student after all (ten years have since passed, so I have a lot to catch up on). On my previous travels I took the time to observe, ask questions, write notes and anecdotes. I thought about my last office job where I composed lengthy sales emails to convince companies to turn down our avenue. I enjoyed writing those – it was the bullshit that I hated. I then found *Lois on the loose, Zen and the Art of Motorcycle Maintenance* and *Jupiter's Travels*. (It wouldn't be a motorbike travelogue if they didn't get a mention.) I decided that I would turn my travel notes into a published memory. One that I would cherish forever. To follow in Granny's footsteps.

Plans took fold. A year-long trip to South America was booked with Tasha, on our own two feet this time. We would travel, volunteer and work our way round. I would take my notes with me, writing in spare moments, like during twenty-plus-hour bus rides through Brazil into Argentina.

Then the Coronavirus pandemic hit.

We were stuck in a one-bedroom flat in Buenos Aires, in a strict lockdown. While everyone was battling over toilet roll in the UK, there wasn't much else for us to do apart from drink delightful Argentinian wine, be merry, and write!

We waited for a repatriation flight home as airlines continued to cancel flights and hold paying customers' money for ransom.

We returned home three months after leaving with a new plan required.

We've since swapped the motorbike for bicycles and cycled around the Western Isles of Scotland. I would recommend taking a trip here in the UK. Something we're going to do more of, reducing the need to fly.

I'll refer back to Edward Abbey's quote at the start of the book: "Save the other half of yourselves and your lives for pleasure and adventure. It is not enough to fight for the land; it is even more important to enjoy it … sit quietly for a while and contemplate the precious stillness, the lovely, mysterious, and awesome space."

I've made some acknowledgements throughout the book but as a final note I would like to say thanks to my family, for your shared support and taught values. I feel very lucky to have you all and all your peculiarities (of which there are many). Thanks to my parents, Liz and Andy, for your continuing generosity and teachings. Thanks for putting us up, and putting up with us throughout the pandemic and also for reading this book a hundred times. Although you're no longer together, you did a bloody good job of bringing us up.

I smoked my last cigarette in Argentina. *That sounds like the title of a new book.*

ABOUT THE ILLUSTRATOR

Aidan Meighan is a cartographer and illustrator living in Somerset who works on personalised map projects for several publications. With a passion for nature and the outdoors, he finds a distinctive style of design for his editorial and custom maps for locations across the globe.

www.whereaboutsmaps.com
Instagram: @whereaboutsmaps

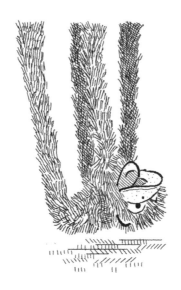

Did you enjoy this book?
Consider writing a review on your favourite website.

Thank you so much for your purchase and support.

www.amerryrideround.com

Lightning Source UK Ltd.
Milton Keynes UK
UKHW051821211122
412578UK00039B/1023